D0852161

1/07/09

To order copies of this publication, please contact:

Health Care Compliance Association
6500 Barrie Road, Suite 250
Minneapolis, MN 55435

Phone: 888-580-8373
Fax: 952-988-0146
e-mail: info@hcca-info.org

Quantity discounts are available.

ISBN 978-0-9778430-0-8

Contents

Glossary terms are bolded the first time they appear in the text.

COMPLIANCE 101

Prologue

PROLOGUE

The field of health care compliance continues to evolve, and we have come a long way since the "big bang" of compliance exploded in 1996. If you are reading this book, you are probably new to the field of compliance. The very first thing you need to know is that you are not alone. With "Compliance Professional" being one of the most sought after professions in the country, many individuals are preparing to enter the field. Let me tell you how I started my career in compliance. I was on vacation in the Great Smoky Mountains late in August 1996, when I received a call from my boss at about 6:00 a.m. That wasn't so unusual, but this time he was calling to ask a special favor. He said, "When you return from vacation I want you to start up a compliance program for us at the University of Louisville." After a moment of shocked silence, I stammered, "But I don't know anything at all about compliance!" "Well," he replied, "Don't tell anyone." I suspect many of you feel you're in the same boat. Your first steps will be the same as mine—education, networking, and on-the-job training.

This book is based on the successful Health Care Compliance Association educational program, Compliance 101. Included will be ideas, tips, and shared impressions from these sessions. There is a glossary at the back of the book as well as sample compliance documents. The primary audience for the book is compliance personnel new to the field, those studying to take the CHC exam or those who would just like a basic refresher. It will also be of value to new compliance committee members, compliance liaisons, and board members. We sincerely hope you will find it helpful.

When I started in compliance in 1996, the literature was not plentiful; educational opportunities were few and far between. Today there are many venues to learn about compliance. Books, newsletters, educational programs, and Web sites abound.

Even when you have an established compliance program up and running, the challenges are not over. At that point you will be looking for ways to re-energize your program. Don't be afraid to network—work with your peers and your colleagues, share information, and help each other. Before you know it, you'll find you're mentoring some new compliance professional who is saying, "But I don't know anything at all about compliance."

Debbie Troklus
Assistant VP Health Affairs/Compliance,
University of Louisville Health Science Center
and President, Healthcare Compliance Certification Board

CHAPTER 1

What's in a Name?

WHAT'S IN A NAME?

You may have noticed that some organizations have **compliance** programs, and others have ethics/integrity programs. They are often considered synonymous but a subtle distinction can be made between the two terms. It is generally thought that the title "compliance program" implies a primary concern with following rules and regulations, whereas the title "integrity program" puts the emphasis on values and doing the right thing. There may be differences in approach and subtleties of content, but there are basic elements common to both compliance and integrity/ethics programs. Those common elements, whatever the title of the program, are the focus of this book, although for convenience sake the term "compliance program" will be used throughout. Each organization must choose a title—or perhaps create an entirely new title—depending on its needs and culture.

You may not be aware of it, but there are probably many compliance activities already occurring in your organization. Things like employment and labor laws, the **Equal Employment Opportunity Commission (EEOC)** and **Employee Retirement Income Security Act (ERISA)** regulations, wage and hour rules, **Occupational Safety and Health Administration (OSHA)**, Nuclear Regulatory Commission requirements, **Joint Commission on Accreditation of Healthcare Organizations (JCAHO)** survey preparation—these are all compliance-related activities. Increasingly, too, academic research is under close compliance scrutiny. Departments coordinating such research activities in your organization should have a compliance-related process dedicated to risks associated with research. This could be a stand-alone compliance program or could be a part of the corporate compliance program.

What Is a Compliance Program?

There are many definitions of a compliance program. On a very basic level, it is about prevention, detection, collaboration, and enforcement. It is a system of policies and procedures developed to assure compliance with and conformity to all applicable federal and state laws governing the organization. A compliance program should not be just a piece of paper or a binder on a shelf; it is not a quick fix to the latest hot problem; it should not be hollow words. A compliance program—an *effective* compliance program—must be an ongoing process, a part of the fabric of the organization, a commitment to an ethical way of conducting business, and a system for doing the right thing.

Who Needs a Compliance Program?

- Physician Practices
- Medicare + Choice Organizations
- Ambulance Suppliers
- Third Party Billing Companies
- Pharmaceutical Manufacturers
- Hospitals
- Laboratories
- Teaching Institutions/Research
- DME Distributors
- Home Health Agencies/Hospices/Nursing Facilities
- Others

So, why do we need yet another program on compliance? Perhaps a little historical perspective is in order. In the 1970s and early 1980s, the Department of Defense was paying exorbitantly high prices for supplies. You may remember the news stories (and the late-night talk show jokes) about $200 hammers and $500 toilet seats. June Gibbs Brown was the **Inspector General (IG)** for the Defense Department at that time. Under her influence, the defense industry suppliers developed voluntary self-regulatory guidelines, called the Defense Industry Initiative, designed to help eliminate waste and bring prices into line. (See the Web site at *www.dii.org*.) Daniel Levinson is the current IG for the **Department of Health & Human Services (HHS)**, and our industry is going through a similar process.

The HHS Office of the Inspector General **(OIG)** in conjunction with the Justice Department is responsible for enforcing the rules and regulations under the Medicare and Medicaid laws outlined as part of the Social Security Act and administered by the Centers for Medicare and Medicaid Services (CMS). Starting in 2003, and each year thereafter, the maximum amount available to OIG for its Health Care Fraud and Abuse Control (HCFAC) Account for Medicare and Medicaid related fraud, waste, and abuse activities is capped at $160 million. In 2005 OIG received $25 million to fight fraud, waste, and abuse associated with the implementation of the Medicare Prescription Drug, Improvement, and Modernization Act. The government estimates of the extent of health care fraud have amounted to approximately 10% of the total U.S. health care expenditures—more than $100 billion annually. In the Justice Department, health care fraud is the number two priority behind violent crime. With health care fraud such a major priority for the government, the stakes are high.

The OIG specifically addresses the benefits of a compliance program in all its program guidances. First and foremost, of course, an effective compliance program safeguards the organization's legal responsibility to abide by applicable laws and regulations. Other important potential benefits identified by the OIG include the ability to:

- Demonstrate to employees and the community the organization's commitment to good corporate conduct
- Identify and prevent criminal and unethical conduct
- Improve the quality of patient care
- Create a centralized source of information on health care regulations
- Develop a methodology that encourages employees to report potential problems
- Develop procedures that allow the prompt, thorough investigation of alleged misconduct
- Initiate immediate and appropriate corrective action
- Reduce the organization's exposure to civil damages and penalties, criminal sanctions, and administrative remedies, such as program exclusion

Another benefit can be found in the OIG Compliance Program Guidance for Hospitals: "Current CMS reimbursement principles provide that certain of the costs associated with the creation of a voluntarily established compliance program may be allowable on certain types of hospitals' costs reports. These allowable costs, of course, must, at a minimum, be reasonable and related to patient care."[1] Not surprisingly, the OIG goes on to point out that costs associated with implementing a government-imposed compliance program, or a **corporate integrity agreement**, are not allowed.

While the cost and the time involved may seem daunting, the cost of not having a compliance program could be higher. An OIG official has allegedly been quoted as saying that you can pay on the front end, or you can pay on the back end. Compliance is not cheap! "While it may require significant additional resources or reallocation of existing resources to implement an effective compliance program," the OIG believes "the long-term benefits of implementing the program outweigh the costs."[2] An effective compliance program is a sound investment.

Why Compliance Programs are Essential

- Paybacks to the fiscal intermediaries or carriers may result in audited services
- Probation and court-imposed programs
- Government-designed programs

- Exclusion from governmental programs
- Reduced threat of **qui tam** (whistle-blower) lawsuits

OIG Top 10 List of Reasons to Implement a Compliance Program

1. **Adopting a compliance program concretely demonstrates to the community at large that a provider has a strong commitment to honesty and responsible corporate citizenship.** One of the company's greatest assets is its reputation; and once damaged, one of the most difficult to repair. An effective compliance program can both preserve and enhance an entity's reputation as a trustworthy provider of **health care**.

2. **Compliance programs reinforce employees' innate sense of right and wrong.** People have an inherent sense of fair play and want a means to respond to conduct they perceive at a gut-level as wrong. A call to the hotline or a review of the compliance manual not only addresses this need, but may identify issues that raise both ethical and legal concerns. By providing employees with ways to express concerns to management and to see a positive response, providers strengthen the relationship of trust with their employees.

3. **An effective compliance program helps a provider fulfill its legal duty to government and private payors.** By submitting a claim for reimbursement for an item or service, the provider affirmatively represents that the claim is truthful and the services were provided consistent with program requirements. As an integral part of the compliance program, internal monitoring of the claims development process helps ensure the accuracy of the provider's submissions.

4. **Compliance programs are cost-effective.** Although an effective compliance program requires a commitment of significant resources, those expenditures are insignificant in comparison to the disruption and expense of defending against a fraud investigation.

5. **A compliance program provides a more accurate view of employee and contractor behavior relating to fraud and abuse.** An effective compliance program provides ongoing training of employees and contractors, monitors their understanding and compliance with program rules, and provides the mechanisms to discipline those individuals who violate the company's code of conduct. It is through these vehicles that a provider can have reasonable assurances that it is acting in conformance with applicable rules.

6. **The quality of care provided to patients is enhanced by an effective compliance program.** As part of a comprehensive compliance program, a code of conduct sets forth the company's vision of itself as a **health care provider**. This vision statement, and its implementation through training of employees, continued self-assessment, and prompt response to identified deficiencies, enhance the provider's ability to deliver health care items or services of the highest quality.

7. **A compliance program provides procedures to promptly correct misconduct.** A comprehensive compliance program provides established procedures for promptly and efficiently responding to problems that may arise. Through early detection and reporting, a company can minimize the loss to the government from false claims, and thereby reduce the provider's exposure to civil damages and penalties, and criminal and administrative sanctions.

8. **An effective compliance program may mitigate any sanction imposed by the government.** Even those companies that implement compliance programs may engage in conduct that violates applicable statutes and regulations. The Organizational Sentencing guidelines of the U.S. Sentencing Commission provide for a reduction in criminal fines in cases where the organization has an effective program to prevent and detect violations of the law. Furthermore, in deciding whether to exclude such a provider from participation in the federal health care programs, the OIG places substantial weight on the existence of an effective compliance program that predates the government's investigation. The standards used by the OIG to evaluate the effectiveness of a compliance program can be found at 62 Fed. Reg. 67393 (December 24, 1997).

9. **Voluntarily implementing a compliance program is preferable to waiting for the OIG to impose a Corporate Integrity Agreement (CIA).** Where a company seeks to resolve its liability for the submission of false claims or other violations of program requirements, the OIG must decide whether the provider should be excluded from the federal health care programs. Generally speaking, the OIG will agree to waive its exclusion authority only if the provider has in place measures that will ensure the abuses will not recur. If the provider does not have an effective compliance program in place, the OIG will develop one that is enforceable under the terms of the corporate integrity agreement. An integrity agreement has detailed policy, training, audit and reporting requirements that are typically in force for five years and involve substantial oversight of the provider by the OIG.

10. **Effective corporate compliance programs may protect corporate directors from personal liability.** The fiduciary duties of corporate directors require that they keep themselves adequately informed concerning the operations of the company. A compliance program designed to assure compliance with applicable legal requirements has been recognized as meeting this duty of care.

Avoidance of penalties and fines can be a major incentive. Should the government find that an organization is guilty of fraud and abuse, the penalties can be severe. The **Health Insurance Portability and Accountability Act of 1996 (HIPAA)** makes it a criminal offense to submit claims based on incorrect codes or medically unnecessary services, and the government has the power to exclude the organization from Medicare, Medicaid, and a long list of other government programs. Indeed, the **Balanced Budget Act of 1997** has a three strikes and you're out clause, requiring permanent expulsion for any health care organization found guilty of fraud a third time. The financial implications due to loss of business can be profound.

Without a compliance program in place, there is also increased threat of qui tam lawsuits. The **False Claims Act (FCA)** empowers the government to investigate and bring civil action in fraud cases. The FCA, implemented during the Civil War to control war-time price gouging, also allows private citizens to bring civil actions against an organization in the name of the United States. The act provides significant financial incentives for private citizens to come forward. Such actions are called qui tam suits. Qui tam is a whistle-blower. The term is abbreviated from the Latin phrase *Qui tam pro domino rege quam pro se ipso in hac parte sequitur*, or "he who brings the action for the king as well as for himself." In health care fraud and abuse actions, the whistle-blower can be eligible to receive anywhere from 15% to 25% of the government's total award for the case if the DOJ decides to assume the case, and 25% to 30% of the total award if the DOJ declines the case. A total of 4,704 qui tam cases were filed between 1987 through September 2004, with total recoveries of $8.45 billion. The total relators' awards when the government pursued the case was $1.33 billion, and when the government declined was $92.1 million. The government has no requirements or expectations about a whistle-blower informing or approaching the organization first, creating a "qui tam paradox." The government promotes an environment of trust where problems are brought forward and resolved; yet whistleblowers are rewarded whether they have tried to solve the problem internally or not. It is not out of the realm of possibility for an organization to hear about an issue for the first time directly from the government.

The government can also impose a CIA against the organization. In order to avoid lengthy and expensive litigation, an organization that negotiates a CIA with the government admits no fault or liability but does submit itself to a government plan for corrective action. Government-imposed CIAs have been onerous in the past—and there is every reason to think they will become more onerous in the future. CIAs have usually had a three- to five-year duration, and some are being extended to eight years. Furthermore, follow-up for CIAs is becoming more severe, with more unannounced audits. Reporting requirements can be extensive. In some cases a government-appointed monitor is put in charge of the organization's compliance program. Paybacks to carriers can result in audited services. Probation also is possible.

So while Corporate Integrity Agreements are government compelled, most compliance programs are better described as "voluntarily mandatory." In a February 27, 1997 open letter to all providers, the OIG encouraged health care organizations to implement compliance programs in order to protect themselves from fraud and abuse. With that letter, the Model Compliance Plan for Clinical Laboratories was offered as guidance. To date, there have been government-released model programs for laboratories, hospitals (along with a supplemental guidance released in 2005), home health, DME (Durable Medical Equipment), hospices, Medicare + Choice, third-party billing companies, individual and small group practices, pharmaceutical manufacturers, ambulance suppliers and nursing facilities.

An organization found guilty of fraud is also subject to fines. In 1984 Congress enacted the Sentencing Reform Act of 1984, which was designed to correct inequities in federal sentences. This legislation includes the **Federal Sentencing Guidelines**, which include guidance for assessing fines and detailed methods for calculation of a **"culpability score."** In 2004 the Federal Sentencing Commission released "Chapter 8 Part B—Remedying Harm from Criminal Conduct, and Effective Compliance and Ethics Program" (viewable at *www.ussc.gov/2004guid/tabconchapt8.htm*). These revisions focused on effective compliance and ethics programs. There are four aggravating factors to a culpability score:

- If an upper-level employee has "participated in, condoned or was willfully ignorant of the offense"
- If the violation is a repeat offense
- If the government was hindered during its investigation and
- If awareness of and tolerance of the violation were pervasive

There are also four mitigating factors:

- If the organization had an effective compliance program, even though there was a violation
- If the organization reported the violation promptly
- If the organization cooperated with the government investigators
- If the organization accepted responsibility for the violation

These factors can have a profound effect on the amount of a fine. They also provide insight into the government approach to compliance programs. Keep in mind that the Federal Sentencing Commission has stated, "Compliance and ethics programs shall be reasonably designed, implemented, and enforced so that the program is generally effective in preventing and detecting criminal conduct. The failure to prevent or detect the instant offense does not necessarily mean that the program is not generally effective in preventing and detecting criminal conduct."

The Hospital Program Guidance states the OIG recognition that there is no "one size fits all" compliance program. It then outlines seven basic elements that can be tailored to fit the needs and financial realities of any given organization. The OIG believes every effective compliance program begins with a formal commitment to these seven basic elements, based on and expanding upon the seven steps of the Federal Sentencing Guidelines. The **seven elements** in the guidance for hospitals, which are consistent with all program guidance, are:

1. Written standards of conduct
2. Designating a chief compliance officer and other appropriate bodies
3. Effective education and training
4. Audits and evaluation techniques to monitor compliance
5. Reporting processes and procedures for complaints
6. Appropriate disciplinary mechanisms
7. Investigation and remediation of systemic problems

All guidances should be read and studied carefully as they make up the backbone of an effective compliance program.

Ten Obstacles to Effective Compliance Implementation
(as compiled from HCCA Compliance 101 educational session participants)

- Commitment and buy-in
- Lack of funding
- Too many roles for compliance professional
- Interpreting laws and regulations
- Lack of resources and staff
- Lack of education and training
- Resistance to change
- Lack of or poor communication
- Fear of retaliation/retribution
- No internal enforcement

CHAPTER 2

The Seven Essential Elements

THE SEVEN ESSENTIAL ELEMENTS

1. Standards of Conduct/Policies and Procedures

In all **OIG program guidances**, the first of the prescribed elements calls for "The development and distribution of written standards of conduct, as well as written policies and procedures that promote [a] . . . commitment to compliance." These two documents, the standards or code of conduct and the policies and procedures, become the tools with which you can build your compliance program.

The standards of conduct, first and foremost, demonstrate the organization's ethical attitude and its "systemwide" emphasis on compliance with all applicable laws and regulations. The code is meant for all employees and all representatives of the organization, not just those most actively involved in compliance issues such as coding and billing. This includes vendors, suppliers, and independent contractors, which are the frequently overlooked groups. From the board to volunteers, everyone must receive, read, understand, and agree to abide by the code of conduct. For this reason the code should be written plainly and concisely in an accessible style. An eighth-grade reading level is recommended. Plain and concise does not mean generic, however. The contents of the code of conduct will need to be tailored to the organization's culture, business, and corporate identity. Also, institutions with a diverse constituency should consider providing the code of conduct in a foreign language, sign language, or even Braille as appropriate.

The code of conduct provides a process for proper decision-making, for doing the right thing. It elevates corporate performance in basic business relationships and confirms that the organization upholds and supports proper compliance conduct. Managers should be encouraged to refer to the code of conduct whenever possible, even incorporating elements or standards into performance reviews. Compliance with the standards must be enforced through appropriate discipline when necessary. Disciplinary procedures should be stated in the standards, and the penalty—up to and including dismissal—for serious violations of the standards of conduct must be mentioned to emphasize the organization's commitment. (See "Enforcement and Discipline," page 34.)

Code of Conduct: Content Checklist

- Demonstrates system-wide emphasis on compliance with all applicable laws and regulations

- Written plainly and concisely so all employees can understand the standards
- Translated into other languages as appropriate
- Includes internal and external regulations
- Mentions organizational policies without completely restating them
- Is consistent with company policies and procedures

Code of Conduct and Employees

- All employees must receive, read, and understand the standards
- A supervisor should explain the standards and answer any questions
- Employees should attest in writing that they have received, read, and understood the standards
- Employee compliance with the standards must be enforced through appropriate discipline when necessary
- Discipline for noncompliance should be stated in the standards

Code of Conduct Purpose

- To present specific guidelines for employees to follow
- To confirm that all employees comprehend what is required of them
- To provide a process for proper decision-making
- To confirm that employees put standards into everyday practice
- To elevate corporate performance in basic business relationships
- To confirm that the organization upholds and supports proper compliance conduct
  (See Appendix A.1, Sample Letter to Vendors.)

Whereas a code of conduct provides guidelines for business decision-making and behavior, the compliance policies and procedures are specific and address identified areas of risk. Most organizations already have an employee manual that outlines all policies and procedures. Whenever possible, compliance policies and procedures should be integrated into existing policies. And while it is imperative that the organization have policies and procedures, it cannot be emphasized enough that **the only thing worse than not having a policy is having a policy and not following it.** Develop your policies and procedures carefully and review them on a regular basis. Take care that they are realistic and measurable. Lofty goals and platitudes may seem appealing but they are too frequently open to interpretation.

Developing your policies and procedures must begin with areas of risk. The OIG Work Plan *(http://www.hhs.gov/progorg/oig)* released in the fall of each year highlights those areas the government will give close attention to in the coming months. Be sure those targeted areas that apply to your organization are adequately addressed in your policies and procedures (and your educational and auditing/monitoring plans). Every health care organization that bills Medicare should also review the compliance Program Guidance for Third-Party Medical Billing Companies for the seventeen billing risk areas and seven coding risk areas, and have compliance policies and procedures for all relevant areas.[3] No matter the size or setting, every organization needs policies and procedures for:

- Internal assessments
- Record retention (where as well as how long)
- Self-disclosure
- Regular Medicare sanction checks (**General Services Administration (GSA)** and OIG sanction lists)
- Billing policies
- **Unbundling**
- Credit balance
- No charge visits
- Incomplete/unsuccessful procedures
- Documentation requirements

The lion's share of fraud and abuse offenses is attributed to documentation and billing irregularities. Medicare in-patient reimbursement is based on the approximately 10,000 numeric codes that make up the ***International Classification of Diseases, 9th Edition, Clinical Modifications*** or **ICD-9-CM**. These codes are organized into **diagnosis related groups (DRGs)**, which form the basis for government payment. The federal government pays a fixed amount according to the assigned diagnosis. This approach, at least in theory, provides incentive to the organization to deliver care as cost effectively as possible.

Some DRGs reimburse at a higher amount than others. A diagnosis of pneumonia with septicemia, for example, will reimburse more than regular pneumonia. **Upcoding** is the practice of using a billing code that provides a higher reimbursement rate than the billing code that actually reflects the service furnished. Upcoding has been a major focus of the OIG's enforcement efforts, and HIPAA added additional **civil monetary penalty** to the OIG's sanction authorities for upcoding violations. The OIG also identifies **DRG creep** as a risk area. DRG creep is the practice of billing using a DRG code that provides a higher payment rate than the DRG code that accurately reflects the service furnished to the patient.

Physician services are described in codes from the ***Current Procedural Terminology 2000*** (**CPT 2000**) published by the American Medical Association.

Submitted codes for physician services must reflect actual services provided. Physicians in teaching situations have additional guidelines. CMS Medicare's Final rule for Teaching Physicians, effective July 1996 and revised in November 2002, outlines documentation regulations for services provided by residents and teaching physicians. Proper documentation of physician supervision of residents is critical in this high-risk area. Billing policies need also to prohibit billing for services never provided and billing for medically unnecessary services.

Lab services pose another risk area to address in policies and procedures. Laboratories are susceptible to extra scrutiny because of the sheer volume of tests performed. Project Bad Bundle was an OIG effort to identify tests processed in groups but reported as processed individually and at the higher rate of reimbursement, also known as unbundling.

There are additional policies and procedures not specifically tied to the OIG Work Plan or OIG Guidances that should be a part of any effective compliance program.

A policy on nonretaliation/nonretribution should be developed and communicated. All employees should understand that they will not be retaliated against for bringing issues forward.

(See Appendix B, Sample Nonretaliation/Nonretribution Policy.)

You must be prepared in the event the government comes knocking at your door. However unlikely, a government investigation is always possible and prior planning is critical. Develop policies so that your staff knows what to do if presented with a search warrant or if questioned by a government investigator. Your organization's counsel should be especially involved in the drafting of these policies. (See Appendix C, Responding to Search Warrant.)

The 72-Hour Window Rule stipulates that diagnostic tests provided on an out-patient basis within 72 hours of admission must be billed as part of the admission DRG. Policies should specify the coding requirements for pre-admission testing and procedures should outline steps to prevent inaccurate billing.

The **anti-kickback statute** prohibits any knowing and willful conduct involving the solicitation, receipt, offer, or payment of any kind of remuneration in return for referring an individual or for recommending or arranging the purchase, lease, or ordering of an item or service that may be wholly or partially paid for under a federal health care program. The anti-kickback statute is a criminal statute. Hefty fines can be levied and, in addition, any reimbursement secured under an illegal referral may be considered a false claim. Potential anti-kickback violations might include offering office space at no charge to physicians, cut-rate support services such as dictation or secretarial services to physicians, or computer equipment provided at no charge by a pharmaceutical company. Be sure you understand the **safe harbors** provided under the anti-kickback statute. A clear, well-publicized policy in support of the anti-kickback statute can prevent confusion and possible problems.

Similarly, the **Stark Laws** apply to physician referrals. The law states that if a physician or a family member has a financial relationship with an entity that provides designated health services (DHS) that the physician may not make a referral for any DHS that is reimbursable by Medicare, and the entity that provides the services may not bill Medicare for the services provided as a result of the prohibited referral. The Stark Act is a civil act, and penalties are substantial. There are exceptions to the Stark statutes, but the regulations are complicated and consulting legal counsel is advised.

Policies and procedures, like the code of conduct, must be living documents, not just a binder on a shelf. They must become integral to the day-to-day operation of the organization. That is what the government will look for. How are the policies and procedures applied every day? Are they incorporated into performance reviews educational programs? Are they reviewed and updated according to a schedule and on time? Revising policies and procedures is something like painting the Golden Gate Bridge; just when you think you're finished, you have to start again at the beginning. You will also need a policy on how and when your review and revision of policies and procedures will be accomplished.

Again, standards of conduct, policies and procedures are the tools of compliance. But they must be used and sharpened to be effective.

2. Compliance Officer and Compliance Committee

The OIG and the Federal Sentencing Guidelines calls for the designation of a compliance professional "to serve as the focal point for compliance activities" (see the OIG's Model Compliance Guidances, and the 2004 revised Federal Sentencing Guidelines). Whether the position is full time or part time will depend on the size, scope, and resources of the institution. Also, according to the OIG, assigning the compliance officer "appropriate authority is critical to the success of the program." The Federal Sentencing Guidelines states, "To carry out such operational responsibility, such individuals shall be given adequate resources, appropriate authority, and direct access to the governing authority or an appropriate subgroup of the governing authority." On a specific level, for example, the compliance officer must have full authority to access any and all documents that are relevant to compliance activities; documents such as patient records, billing records, contracts with suppliers, agents, and hospital-based physicians. But in the big picture, "appropriate authority" comes from the unquestionable backing of the board of directors or its equivalent, the source of the respect that will get things done.

Appropriate authority and the full backing of the board of directors and management are consistent with the OIG's call for the appointment of a "high-level official . . . with direct access to the governing body, the CEO, all other senior management and legal counsel."[4] This is logical because it is the board that launched the compliance initiative and approved the hiring of the compliance officer. Board members may even have been actively involved in the interviewing and hiring of the compliance officers. They should also have been involved in the drafting—certainly the reviewing—of the compliance officer's job description. And they will be an important part of the compliance officer's reporting structure.

The OIG considers there to be some risk involved in having the compliance officer report to general counsel or to the chief financial officer. Some liken this reporting arrangement to the fox minding the chicken coop. Separation of compliance from legal and finance when possible, the OIG argues, helps ensure that legal reviews and financial analyses are independent and objective. According to a 2005 HCCA survey, the results of which were published as the HCCA's 2005 Profile of Health Care Compliance Officers, reporting structure varies depending on the size of the organization. Most compliance officers report directly to the organization CEO and/or the board.

Compliance Officer Reporting Structures Based on Size of Organization

| | | | NUMBER OF EMPLOYEES | | | | | | | |
| | All Respondents | | Less Than 1,000 | | 1,000 to 2,999 | | 3,000 to 4,999 | | 5,000 or More | |
	#	%	#	%	#	%	#	%	#	%
To whom does the Compliance Officer directly report?										
Number of Respondents	627	100	228	100	180	100	79	100	122	100
CEO/President	393	63	143	63	121	67	57	72	63	52
Board	255	41	96	42	66	37	39	49	50	41
CFO/Finance	77	12	21	9	31	17	13	16	9	7
VP Level	59	9	15	7	20	11	11	14	13	11
COO	37	6	15	7	10	6	4	5	8	7
Academic Executive	13	2	5	2	2	1	0	0	5	4
Legal	44	7	8	4	13	7	6	8	16	13
Legal	44	7	8	4	13	7	6	8	16	13
Audit Committee	46	7	1	0	15	8	14	18	16	13
Finance Committee	12	2	1	0	4	2	3	4	4	3
Compliance Committee	89	14	26	11	34	19	9	11	19	16
Other Committee	3	0	1	0	2	1	0	0	0	0
Internal Audit	5	1	0	0	3	2	1	1	1	1
Administrator/Executive Director	36	6	22	10	4	2	1	1	8	7
Chief Compliance Officer	39	6	13	6	10	6	3	4	8	7
Risk Management	6	1	3	1	2	1	1	1	0	0

The size and setting of your organization will influence its reporting structure. It is recommended that the board or its liaison committee have, at minimum, a "dotted line" or indirect reporting relationship with the compliance officer.

The compliance officers' duties also will vary depending on size and scope of the program. The main focus of the position should be the implementation, administration and oversight of the compliance program. Primary responsibilities, according to the OIG, should include:

- Overseeing and monitoring the implementation of the compliance program
- Reporting on a regular basis to the governing body, CEO, and compliance committee
- Revising the compliance program periodically as appropriate
- Developing, coordinating, and participating in a multifaceted educational and training program
- Ensuring that independent contractors and agents are aware of the organization's compliance program requirements
- Ensuring that appropriate background checks are done to eliminate sanctioned individuals and contractors
- Assisting with internal compliance review and monitoring activities
- Independently investigating and acting on matters related to compliance

Health care compliance is evolving as a profession. Education and skill sets vary among those who have chosen compliance as their profession. The most recent **Health Care Compliance Association** survey (2005) found that among its members responding to the survey, 31% held bachelor's degrees, 29% had master's degrees, 20% were attorneys (Juris Doctorate), 16% were MBA's, 16% were CHC's, 10% were RNs/ Nursing, 8% CPAs, 5% associate degree, 3% no degree, 3% doctorate, and 3% MD/DO. (Note percentages do not total 100% because some respondents listed more than one degree.) When asked the number of people in this role previously within the same organization, 90% reported none in 1999 (due to many being just in the implementation process) and in 2005 the number decreased to 48% (demonstrating the maturity of some programs).[5] Whatever the tenure or the educational level, the compliance officer as "focal point" of the program must be a figure respected and trusted throughout the organization. Strong interpersonal skills, good listening abilities, and discretion are mandatory. (See Appendix D, Compliance Officer Job Description.)

As compliance has grown and matured as a profession, it has, like other professions, sought to identify and distinguish those in the field who have, with experience and education, achieved the necessary skill set to be an effective compliance officer. Through rigorous testing, HCCA's credentialing program, administered by the Health Care Compliance Board (HCCB), identifies and certifies those who can meet such high standards of expertise. The letters CHC after a compliance professional's name indicates that he or she is thoroughly knowledgeable in all areas of compliance. Becoming certified in healthcare compliance (CHC) is becoming a goal of many compliance professionals and is being requested as a job requirement by many organizations.

Moreover, like all health care professionals, compliance officers are also stewards of a public trust and therefore the services provided must be of the highest standards of professionalism, integrity, and competence. The Health Care Compliance Association has prepared and published the Code of Ethics for Health Care Compliance Professionals (see Appendix J). This document addresses three principles, which are broad standards of an aspirational and inspirational nature. They include:

Principle I: Obligations to the Public—Health care compliance professionals should embrace the spirit and the letter of the law governing their employing organization's conduct and exemplify the highest ethical standards in their conduct in order to contribute to the public good.

Principle II: Obligations to the Employing Organization—Health care compliance professionals should serve their employing organizations with the highest sense of integrity, exercise unprejudiced and unbiased judgment on their behalf, and promote effective compliance programs.

Principle III: Obligation to the Profession—Compliance professionals should strive, through their actions, to uphold the integrity and dignity of the profession, to advance the effectiveness of compliance programs and to promote professionalism in health care compliance.

These principles and the accompanying Rules of Conduct should be reviewed and studied—and adhered to—by all compliance officers.

The compliance officer may be the "focal point" of a compliance program, but he or she cannot be the only point. The OIG also urges a compliance committee be established "to advise the compliance officer and assist in the implementation of the compliance program."[6] Although there is no specific direction about the composition of the committee, the OIG does note that the committee will benefit from having varying perspectives "such as operations, finance, audit, human resources, utilization review, social work, discharge planning, medicine, coding and legal, as well as employees and managers of key operating units"[7] (see the *OIG Compliance Program Guidance for Hospitals, II.B.2.,* footnote 39, 1998). It will serve the organization well to a have a physician representative.

The compliance officer's role with the compliance committee can vary. In some organizations the CO sits *ex officio*. In others, the CO may even chair the committee. The HCCA 2005 Profile of Health Care Compliance Officers reports that in 78% of organizations responding to the HCCA Survey the compliance officer oversees the compliance committee and meets either monthly or quarterly. Physicians are strong leaders in the health care field and so other organizations may have a physician chair of the committee. No matter who chairs the committee, the compliance department will in all likelihood be responsible for scheduling meetings, preparing the agenda, taking and distributing minutes, and coordinating follow-up.

The compliance committee has many functions in addition to aiding and supporting the compliance officer. They include:

- Analyzing legal requirements and specific risk areas
- Regularly reviewing and assessing policies and procedures
- Assisting with the development of standards of conduct and policies and procedures
- Monitoring internal systems related to standards, policies and procedures
- Determining the appropriate strategy to promote compliance
- Developing a system to solicit, evaluate, and respond to complaints and problems

The importance and potential influence of the compliance committee cannot be understated. Look for committed individuals who will be strong, visible, and vocal advocates for the compliance program.

3. Education

Education and training are the first and possibly the most important lines of defense for a compliance program. In a field where the pages of regulations number in the thousands, education is the best strategy for prevention. The revised Federal Sentencing Guidelines and all OIG model guidance identify the need for education and training. The *Compliance Program Guidance for Third-Party Medical Billing Companies* states, "The proper education and training of corporate officers, managers, employees, and the continual retraining of current personnel at all levels, are significant elements of an effective compliance program."[8] The OIG suggests training be separated into two sessions: the first a general session on compliance for all employees and the second covering more specific information for appropriate personnel.

Ten Things to Include in Your Basic Compliance Course[9]

1. The body of legal and regulatory knowledge guiding all compliance activity
2. Your organization's specific compliance philosophy
3. How to handle compliance communication within and outside of your organization
4. How compliance violations are defined and how they should be reported

5. Policies regarding patient confidentiality handling of patient-specific information
6. Claims submission—the activity most at risk for compliance exposure
7. Only qualified individuals will be permitted to perform diagnosis and procedure coding
8. Physician documentation is the primary determinant of claim submission
9. Vendors will be held to the same compliance standards as staff
10. Employees involved in compliance violations will be disciplined

General training sessions are meant to heighten awareness among all employees and communicate and emphasize (and then update and reiterate) the organization's commitment to ethical business behavior, which effects all employees. The OIG urges that employees be required to have a specific number of educational hours per year, as appropriate. For a frame of reference, a minimum of one to three hours annually for basic training in compliance areas is required in many corporate integrity agreements. As noted earlier, all employees should receive a copy of the standards of conduct. These, plus basic information about the organization's compliance program and how it operates, are the core of general training.

Specific training in high-risk areas is critical for specialized personnel. Review of the most recent OIG Work Plan is a good start not only for initial training but for refresher courses as well. Claims submission has been at the heart of most settlements to date, and education related to this area of compliance should be emphasized. The Federal Sentencing Commission and the OIG recommend training for appropriate corporate officers, managers, and other staff on such topics as:

- Ethics
- Government and private payor reimbursement principles
- General prohibitions on paying or receiving remuneration to induce referrals
- Proper confirmation of diagnoses
- Submitting a claim for physician services when rendered by a non-physician
- Signing a form for a physician without the physician's authorization
- Alterations to medical records
- Prescribing medications and procedures without proper authorization
- Proper documentation of services rendered
- Duty to report misconduct

The OIG notes, "Clarifying and emphasizing these areas of concern through training and educational programs are particularly relevant to a hospital's marketing and financial personnel, in that the pressure to meet business goals may render these employees vulnerable to engaging in prohibited practices."[10]

A written annual education plan should outline individual department content needs, timing, methods and duration of training, and a strategy for securing managerial buy-in. An uncooperative manager can, directly or indirectly, consciously or unconsciously, deter staff from attending. The manager must emphasize the importance of training by encouraging and *facilitating* employee attendance. That may mean juggling schedules or requiring others to "pick up the slack" during education sessions when a unit may be left shorthanded. Consulting with managers in advance about content needs and especially timing issues can prevent conflicting priorities later. Also, inviting management to participate in the planning will help to give them ownership, which helps to promote buy-in for the educational activity.

Adult learning styles vary. Some learn through listening, others through seeing, and many by doing. So, to keep education vital and engaging to a diversified staff, the key is to develop a variety of educational formats: videos, lectures, brown bag lunches, physician/roundtable discussions. Brown bag lunches and roundtable discussion can be especially effective in targeting a specific training need. Your organization may already have various forums you can tap into for targeted education, such as department meetings or all-staff meetings. Look for ways to integrate compliance education into other scheduled training sessions; integrate compliance into what you're doing now so that it blends with the fabric of the organization. Shadowing providers can be an effective method of training on effective documentation techniques. The compliance officer or designee "shadows" the physician for a day in order to provide input on documentation and to answer questions. When training providers be sure to address both the business and clinical sides of the issue. For example, the business side is correct documentation for correct reimbursement, the clinical side is quality of care and continuity.

Training Adult Learners[11]

- Acknowledge "life learning"
- Acknowledge self-worth
- Associate the unfamiliar with the familiar
- Recognize individual resourcefulness
- Do not treat as prisoners
- Teach to all types of adult learning styles
    - Those who learn through listening (use active repetition, songs, skits, etc.)
    - Those who learn through seeing (use handouts, videos, etc.)
    - Those who learn by doing (use hands-on projects, role-playing, etc.)

Should compliance education be voluntary or mandatory? The OIG guidance says that at the end of general training, every employee, as well as contracted consultants, should be required to sign and date a statement that confirms his or her knowledge of and commitment to the standards of conduct. This **attestation**, according to the OIG, is to be retained in the employee's personnel file. Each organization must decide how ardently to pursue 100% attestation. While mandatory may be the OIG's and the compliance officer's preference, it is often the more difficult route. The challenge comes with the outliers, the last 5% who just can't seem to get to the training sessions no matter how many opportunities you offer. How many reminders can you send? Is 100% attendance even achievable?

Sample Attestation/Acknowledgement Form

This is to acknowledge that I have received and reviewed [Hospital Name's] *Code of Conduct*. I agree to comply with the standards contained in the code and all related policies and procedures as is expected as part of my continued employment or association with the organization. I acknowledge that the code is only a statement of principles for individual and business conduct, and does not constitute an employment contract. I will report any potential violation of which I become aware promptly to my supervisor or the compliance officer. I understand that any violation of the Code of Conduct or any corporate compliance policy or procedures is grounds for disciplinary action, up to and including discharge from employment.

_____   _____

Date   *Name (Please Print) / Signature*

Compliance programs are ongoing and evolving. Educational opportunities have become more and more plentiful and easier to attend, and word has spread about their value. Ultimately, those who attend realize it benefits them as well as the organization. While 100% attendance may be difficult to achieve, reticent staff should be prompted to participate. Personal notes about upcoming education sessions to those who have avoided training in the past can help. A note or a personal call to a supervisor asking for support can be effective as well. Ultimately, the goal is to show improvement in educational attendance.

Other organizations take a harder line. At the University of Louisville School of Medicine, for example, training is offered free of charge for two months. During that time Web-based educational sessions are available 24/7. But for those who choose not to take the online training during those two months, in the third month their department is billed $100 for the same training that would have been "free" the previous month. In the fourth month the charge goes up to $200. This strategy can be very effective but it does require the support of executive staff and the finance office. With this system, at the end of the fourth month all billing is suspended until the provider is compliant with training. Amazingly, this method has worked, and they are obtaining 100%.

The benefits of compliance education and training must be communicated from the top. Attendance by top management, especially at an annual basic program, sends a powerful message. If the CEO can make time, others will follow suit. Other incentives include multiple offerings at alternative times to facilitate attendance. Also, consider the time commitment involved. Everyone today is too busy. Explore with unit managers the pros and cons of two one-hour sessions versus one two-hour session, for example. Also, you may need to give thought to the method of training. Web-based training is a very popular method and can address the timing issue since individuals can take it whenever it is convenient for them. One disadvantage is that there is not an opportunity to discuss. Food, even simple fare such as doughnuts, however trite it may sound, does serve as an incentive. Achieving 100% attendance will never be easy. You will need to be creative to find ways to motivate voluntary attendance.

It should be clear by now that compliance cannot be a one-shot educational event. Your compliance committee can help in assessing the best approach on such issues as whether to make education mandatory or voluntary and how to structure education and training options within the organization. Again, your organization's culture is the driving force. Education and training are your best strategies for prevention—and the old adage still rings true, an ounce of prevention is worth a pound of cure. Remember to attend to your own educational needs as well. The more you know, the better you can identify and meet the educational needs of staff.

4. Monitoring and Auditing

An effective compliance program is one with a process of constant evaluation. No one can expect 100% compliance from the first day. The key is to strive for and demonstrate a process for continually improving on compliance activities. The OIG's emphasis on the importance of evaluation is evident in that all corporate integrity agreements call for regular monitoring at least annually. Moreover, all OIG compliance program guidance states that ongoing evaluation is critical to a successful compliance program.

The OIG calls for audits to focus on programs or divisions, including external relations with third-party contractors, especially those with substantive exposure to government enforcement action. There are certain functions common to all types of organizations that should be reviewed:

- Anti-kickback and self-referral issues
- Credit balances
- Bad debts
- Claim development and submission
- Record retention
- Cost reporting
- Marketing
- Compliance program processes

Other functions to be reviewed will depend on the type of organization. For example, a teaching hospital should look at compliance with the teaching regulations. Clinical laboratories will want to review physician requisition procedures. Audits should also take into account the organization's compliance in relation to the OIG Work Plan and any relevant OIG Fraud Alerts. And obviously, any areas of concern previously identified either internally or by an outside agency should be looked at carefully as well.

There are at least two ways to approach auditing: the **concurrent audit** and the **retrospective audit**. Every organization is unique and, again, you must do what is best for your organization, but in most cases retrospective audits are not recommended.

A retrospective audit will provide a broad baseline risk assessment, a **snapshot**, or essentially a laundry list of all the things you need to fix. However unlikely, if the OIG does knock on your door, you have everything nicely itemized for its investigators. Moreover, it is at best optimistic to think that one can identify in some finite period of time everything that could possibly be wrong and then try to set up a realistic time frame for addressing those problems. There is only so much that can be done in a day, and the rules keep changing as well. Better to identify a problem and fix it. Organizations need to understand their risk areas and have a plan on how to manage them.

A concurrent audit will identify and address potential problems individually as they arise. If there is indeed an issue, then correct the related policy or procedure if applicable, communicate the change and then go back in, say, three months and perhaps again in six months, to review and be sure the issue is resolved.

A note of caution. If you do a retrospective audit and you discover billing errors, you are required to report the errors and pay back any amount due the government. No matter what the circumstances, if you find you actually are doing something wrong, especially if money is involved, you are strongly encouraged to contact your **fiscal intermediary (FI)** or your carrier. The problem should be reported and any overpayments will need to be refunded. As soon as you suspect there is the possibility of wrongdoing, the first step is to contact your in-house or external counsel, who can make an initial assessment of the risk involved. Your counsel too will instruct you as to whether investigations should continue under **attorney-client privilege**.

Monitoring, or regular review, is also necessary to determine whether compliance elements, such as dissemination of standards, training, and disciplinary action, have been satisfied. It will also target potential deficiencies and areas where modifications might be in order. A good place to begin an internal assessment is by interviewing employees. They are a wealth of knowledge. Ask them openly about risk, about their daily activities, the processes, procedures, and whether these methods are sound. Ask if the policies and procedures are followed. Periodically send out questionnaires to staff for feedback or conduct focus groups. Set up systems for regular and sometimes random review of medical and financial records, especially written documentation. Data collection and tracking are the heart and soul of review because they provide trend analysis and a measure of progress. The OIG recommends the compliance officer or reviewer consider the following techniques:

- On-site visits
- Interviews with personnel involved in management, operations, coding, claim development and submission, patient care, and other related activities
- Questionnaires developed to solicit impressions of a broad cross-section of the hospital's employees and staff
- Reviews of written medical and financial records and other source documents that support claims for reimbursement and Medicare Cost reports
- Reviews of written materials and documentation prepared by the different divisions of a hospital
- Trend analyses, or longitudinal studies, that seek deviations, positive or negative, in specific areas over a given period
- Including compliance language in job descriptions and job evaluations
- Posing compliance-related questions in exit interviews

Sample Compliance-Related Exit Interview Questions
Responses to these questions should be reported to the compliance officer.

- How do you feel about communications in your unit? How about communications overall?
- How do you think the organization lives up to its code of conduct?

- Did you have any concerns about ethical issues or compliance-related practices? If so, please explain.
  (See Appendix E, Compliance Audit Review Form.)

Who is responsible for coordinating the monitoring and conducting the internal audit? Is this an internal auditor's responsibility or the compliance office's responsibility, or perhaps a combination of the two? First, to avoid duplication or overlap, consider if there are other departments in your organization doing auditing. Start with the finance department and the regular financial statement audits usually provided by outside certified public accountant consultants. Also, quality improvement or quality assurance activities are usually underway at all levels of the organization. These activities can dovetail with the monitoring and auditing elements of an effective compliance program. Auditors will need experience in the area they are observing. For instance, nurses or physicians should review charts for medical necessity. Certified coders should review documentation and coding. And to assure objectivity, reviewers should be independent of physicians and line management. It is also important that they have access to existing audit and health care resources and relevant personnel. If you have in-house coders checking other in-house coders, be sure there are checks and balances in place. Consider internal ad hoc groups—compliance SWAT teams—to monitor specific issues or review potential problem areas. References should be carefully checked for any outside auditors employed by the organization.

Any questions posed to or communications with the FI will be taken into account in an audit or review. The larger your organization, the greater the difficulty in documenting such contacts. Be sure to take notes when you have a telephone conversation with an FI or a carrier representative. Ask for written confirmation of the information provided, but always keep your own notes of the conversation, including the date, time, and contact name as well as the specifics of the conversation. As a preventive measure, in some organizations the billing manager meets periodically with the FI or the carrier representative to discuss industry issues as well as specific questions. Such meetings build better communication lines and enhance understanding of expectations and requirements.

Audits and reviews must be documented and reported. The OIG calls for regular reporting to senior company officers. For example, the OIG hospital guidance calls for written evaluations to be presented to the CEO, governing body, and members of the compliance committee no less than annually. The *Program Guidance for Third-Party Medical Billing Companies* adds that when a facility is part of a larger corporate entity, monitoring and auditing activities should be a key feature of any annual review.[12] Appropriate reports on audit findings should be periodically provided and explained to a parent organization's senior staff and officers.[13]

Reports to management, the governing body, and the compliance committee should include findings or suspicions of misconduct with an action plan to address and resolve the potential problem.

5. Reporting and Investigating

There are a variety of methods for employees to report potential problems or to raise concerns. The OIG stresses the importance of communication in the compliance process: "An open line of communication between the compliance officer and . . . personnel is equally important to the successful implementation of a compliance program and the reduction of any potential fraud, abuse and waste"[14] (see the OIG's Compliance Program Guidance for Home Health Agencies, II.D.1. or other OIG model compliance programs). The most important reporting system is an open door, and the best reporting system is one where the employee feels comfortable approaching his or her supervisor and openly discussing any potential problem.

For any reporting method to be effective, employees must accept that there will be no retaliation or retribution for coming forward. The concept of nonretaliation is fundamental to the compliance program, and a clearly stated policy regarding nonretribution is the first step. (See Appendix B: Sample Nonretaliation/Nonretribution Policy.) The dangers are real. If employees suspect there could be retaliation, no one will come forward, creating fertile ground for whistle-blowers.

Confidentiality is also key. Policies and procedures should assure, to the extent possible, confidentiality and anonymity in all reporting processes. (See Appendix F: Sample Confidentiality Statement.) Confidentiality is, of course, closely tied with nonretaliation. For example, the decision-making process regarding a promotion can be tainted if the supervisor has been informed of an employee-candidate's report of a problem. Policies and procedures need to offer assurances to the employee but must also note that resolution of a problem, which could include legal action, may in certain circumstances require disclosure of identity. Legal counsel should review both the nonretaliation and confidentiality policies to be sure unrealistic promises are not made.

One common reporting method recommended by the OIG is the **hotline** or **helpline**. There are various arguments for whether to handle a hotline internally or externally. The size and setting of the organization must factor into the decision. A large organization may need 24-hour coverage. For a smaller organization, 24-hour coverage may not be needed or may only be feasible through outsourcing, which can be costly. Also, cost and resources needed for training staff on how to handle calls and protect confidentiality must be weighed against the costs of professional, albeit possibly expensive, telephone services. If you decide to outsource, the contract should include:

- The right to move the toll-free number to another vendor or bring it in-house
- A requirement that the vendor check names mentioned in the call against the HHS-IG and the GSA list of excluded individuals (providing a check on internal processes)
- Assurances that security of the vendor computer system equals the security provided for the data within your own system
- An electronic method of linking the incoming phone line with the computer of the person answering the call (to decrease the risk of your hotline calls being routed, even inadvertently, to another client of the vendor)

Whether you handle your hotline internally or whether you outsource, anonymity must be promised to the extent possible. Hotline numbers and procedures must be clearly and readily communicated to staff, preferably not solely through a page in the employee policies and procedures manual. Permanent and prominent bulletin board postings ensure that everyone knows problems are to be reported and that they understand how to report a problem or a question.

Once you have a hotline up and running, how do you assess its effectiveness? Do frequent calls necessarily indicate an effective hotline? Not necessarily. If you have been able to create an environment where issues are raised through appropriate channels, where staff members trust that they can report problems without fear of retaliation, you may not get a lot of calls. Also, approximately 80% of hotline calls are human resources or employer-relations issues—complaints about a supervisor's behavior or a colleague's allegedly insulting remark, or disagreements with the organization's policy on overtime, for example. Here again, consider your organization's culture. The number of calls alone, however, is not an indicator of effectiveness.

Once a complaint is received or a question raised, it must be investigated. Remember, to the government, documentation is everything. All complaints must be logged in and tracked. Many organizations assign a unique number to each call so that the caller can check on the status of the complaint by calling back and giving the assigned number. How the complaint was handled, by whom, and when should all be included in the documentation. (See Appendix G, Compliance Line Information.) The log sheet should also be supplemented with a complaint-specific issue form. Noting that a complaint was received is not enough. Documentation of the specifics of the issue, the department(s) involved, findings, and actions taken is also necessary. (See Appendix H, In-Take Form and Case Disposition Log.) You also need a clearly stated procedure outlining the disposition of these forms, specifically who gets copies and how information is incorporated into written reports.

There should also be a written policy and procedure regarding how calls to the hotline, or input to any reporting mechanism for that matter, will be addressed. Specific steps for an investigation should be enumerated and such a policy must limit distribution of information to protect confidentiality and nonretaliation commitments. Hotlines can seem like a sizeable expense, but in many organizations, if not most, they are a practical investment. The employee's options shouldn't be limited to 1-800-HHS-TIPS.

In addition to hotlines, some organizations have in-house e-mail systems. With the help of the information services department, e-mail can be configured so that problems can be reported but the compliance officer cannot determine who is sending the e-mail. In today's work environment, computers are commonplace, but they are not ubiquitous. Some jobs do not require a desk with access to a computer, and a centrally located general-access terminal could compromise confidentiality. For these reasons, e-mail probably shouldn't be the only reporting system. If adopting this sort of system as part of your reporting options, however, remember to emphasize in your procedures that anyone who *does* want to hear back will need to include his or her name in the body of the e-mail since there will be no way for the compliance officer to know who sent the e-mail.

Another reporting option is a drop box, a variation on the old suggestion box. Regular and frequent pick-ups will be important, and multiple locations are encouraged—although be sure not to position it in an area of the institution with a security camera.

Reporting works both ways, of course, and the compliance officer should take every opportunity to keep in touch with all levels of staff. Regular ongoing communication is another form of education that reiterates commitment and can facilitate prevention of problems. Compliance communication can be incorporated into existing systems: a compliance column of frequently asked questions in the organization's in-house newsletter, posters on bulletin boards, tent cards in the cafeteria. Good channels for communication must be in place and effective when changes or additions to policy or procedures occur. You may consider a fax alert system for special announcements. Use urgent fax alerts sparingly, however; otherwise they will risk not being taken seriously. Save such alerts for an OIG advisory opinion, for example, or, if you are a teaching hospital, a new development related to teaching physician requirements. Whatever communication you do, be sure to keep copies in a binder or file so you can document what you are communicating, how, to whom, and when. All-staff e-mails, articles in the in-house newsletter, a page on the company intranet, brief presentations at all staff meetings—all these methods of communication will reinforce the message that the compliance department is available to staff.

6. Enforcement and Discipline

Fair, equitable, and consistent are the watchwords for enforcing the standards of conduct and the policies and procedures. The place to start with enforcement is back at the beginning with the standards of conduct and the policies and procedures. The OIG believes that the compliance program should include a written policy statement setting forth the degrees of disciplinary actions that may be imposed upon corporate officers, managers, employees, physicians, and other health care professionals for failing to comply with standards, policies and applicable statutes and regulations. That policy should include five points:

- Noncompliance will be punished
- Failure to report noncompliance will be punished
- An outline of disciplinary procedures
- The parties responsible for appropriate action
- A promise that discipline will be fair and consistent

It is important to emphasize that "sins of omission" as well as "sins of commission" will be subject to discipline. Failure to detect or report an offense is a serious act of noncompliance and equally as deserving of discipline as the actual misconduct. Compliance is an active, on-going process that is everyone's responsibility.

In this area you are well-advised to consult closely with the organization's Human Resources (HR) department. There are no doubt disciplinary policies and procedures already in place with which you will need to be consistent, and which can serve as a model. One important piece of advice your HR colleagues will probably give you is that you cannot discipline without having properly informed all employees of the rules. Although stated earlier, it bears reiteration here too—the policies and procedures must be clear and they must be appropriately communicated to all staff. It is much more difficult to penalize someone for violating a policy he or she did not know about. Hence, the first step toward enforcement is distributing standards of conduct and policies and procedures and educating staff about them, including the consequences of noncompliance.

The OIG calls for the written standards of conduct to address the procedures for handling disciplinary problems and those who will be responsible for taking appropriate action. Intentional or reckless noncompliance is to be punishable with "significant sanctions," which can range from oral warnings to suspension, privilege revocation (subject to any applicable peer review procedures), termination or financial penalties as appropriate. Many organizations use progressive discipline. As the name implies, this is a multi-step process where the penalties become increasingly more severe. The first step in this process should be a supervisor's conference. The goal of the supervisor's conference is to secure the employee's understanding of the problem and a commitment to correcting the inappropriate behavior. Depending on the situation, the next step might be a conference with a higher level of authority, or it could be a written warning. The written warning is the more severe next step, and it emphasizes the seriousness of the situation and stresses the urgency of modified behavior. It should also outline that the employee will face further disciplinary action, up to and including termination, if the problem behavior continues. Subsequent steps might include suspension without pay or infliction of a probationary period where the employee is advised to correct the behavior within a certain time period, say 30 days, or face termination. The final step is termination once all other options have been exhausted. The severity of the infraction will determine the steps. Certainly, any step beyond the basic supervisor's conference should involve the HR department. Proper and properly thorough documentation will be essential.

Punishment should be commensurate with the offense. There are offenses such as blatant acts of fraud that warrant immediate termination. But most infractions will be relatively minor and most likely unintentional. These may best be handled with education or additional training. Education should never be labeled as "punishment"; put in a positive and supportive context, it can efficiently correct noncompliant behavior. Be sure your policies and procedures include remedial steps such as additional training.

In the context of enforcing standards, the OIG also urges a "new employee policy," which applies particularly to those who have the authority to make decisions regarding compliance issues or supervise those who do. The organization is urged to do "a reasonable and prudent background investigation, including reference check" as part of the application process. Include review of the federal health care sanctions lists as part of this investigation. Also, the application form itself should ask the applicant to note any incidents of criminal conviction or exclusion action. This proactive strategy can prevent hiring a sanctioned individual (itself prohibited by the OIG). Such cautions apply to contracts with outside vendors as well. A footnote in the Hospital Guidance calls for compliance programs to "establish standards prohibiting the execution of contracts with companies that have been recently convicted of a criminal offense related to health care,"[16] or which have been determined to be ineligible to participate in federal health care programs.

Enforcement is not just about discipline, of course. Goals and objectives for individuals and departments can include specific references to compliance. Achievement of those goals, especially when celebrated, is a positive reinforcement that encourages support for and enforcement of the compliance program. Performance appraisals need not focus solely on issues of noncompliance. They can, for example, make note of favorable or improved audit or review outcomes. Your compliance program can be better enforced if you also find ways to reinforce with positive feedback.

7. Response and Prevention

If there should ever be reason to believe that misconduct or wrongdoing has actually occurred, the organization must respond appropriately. Failure to respond or to engage in lengthy delay can have serious consequences. The OIG notes that violations of the compliance program and other types of misconduct threaten an organization's status as a reliable, honest, and trustworthy provider capable of participating in federal health care programs. Detected but uncorrected misconduct can seriously endanger the mission, reputation, and legal status of the hospital. Ignoring a legitimate report of wrongdoing will also alienate staff, especially the person who reported the problem, and hence encourage qui tam action. Cover-ups usually cause more problems than they solve. In the event of misconduct, face the problem and fix it. However daunting it may feel to be faced with the possibility of misconduct, remember that one of the goals of a compliance program is *detection*. Having found a problem is an indication your program is working.

The first logical step is to meet with your in-house or external legal counsel. Together you can determine how serious the misconduct or wrongdoing is and develop an appropriate plan of action. The OIG recommends an investigation any time a potential violation is identified. Therefore, your plan of action will likely begin with a thorough *internal investigation*. Depending on the extent and seriousness of the alleged infraction, outside counsel or content experts may be needed. Your counsel will help decide whether the investigation should be handled under the attorney-client privilege. With *attorney-client privilege*, disclosure communications and most documents can be kept in confidence. While an internal investigation is the first step, be sure to take the necessary steps immediately to stop or modify the procedures that are the alleged source of wrongdoing.

The internal investigation must be handled carefully and documented meticulously. When choosing an investigative team, look for those knowledgeable about the area in question but also capable of being objective. The compliance officer should obviously be a part of the team, but to emphasize commitment, participation by a member of the senior staff is desirable when possible. If outside consultants are used, the compliance office must still be represented on the team. Handing the problem off to someone else is not a solution. Outside consultants will need to be directed, overseen, and evaluated just as closely as an internal investigation team, if not more so. The team should meet together as a group in the beginning to delineate the problem, decide on an approach or strategy, and get the guidance and support of senior management. Instructions on timeframe, process, and the need for documentation are also in order. At minimum, the team should meet together again as a group at the end of the investigative process to discuss findings and plan the final report. Time is of the essence. The OIG calls for prompt reporting of misconduct to the appropriate governmental authority within a reasonable period, but not more than 60 days after determining that there is credible evidence of a violation and not more than 30 days to avoid stricter fines.

As noted above, detailed documentation is critical. If it should be necessary to defend in a criminal or civil trial, a clear paper trail will make the process much easier. Thorough documentation will include:

- A description of the potential misconduct and how it was reported
- A description of the investigative process
- List of relevant documents reviewed
- List of employees interviewed
- Employee interview questions and notes
- Changes to policies and procedures, if appropriate
- Documentation of any disciplinary actions
- Investigation final report with recommended remedial actions

The final report and any attached documentation are sensitive materials and should be distributed in limited quantities.

If the investigation finds that there was no violation, all is well. However, if after the internal investigation there is reason to believe the organization misconduct constituted a material violation of the civil law or the rules and regulations governing federally funded heath care programs, then the organization must take steps to disclose the violation to the government. Per the OIG, "As appropriate, such steps may include an immediate referral to criminal and/or civil enforcement authorities, a corrective action plan, a report to the Government, and the submission of any overpayments, if applicable" *(see the OIG Compliance Program Guidance for Hospitals, II.G.2., 1998).*[17]

Voluntary disclosure is not only the right thing to do, it also provides certain financial advantages. Those who violate the False Claims Act are liable to the government for civil penalty of not less than $5,000 and not more than $10,000, plus treble damages sustained by the government, for each false claim filed. If the organization reports the violation within 30 days of discovery, however, damages can be significantly reduced. Also, if an organization itself is the first to report the violation, a *qui tam* action is less likely.

The OIG encourages voluntary disclosure of suspected fraud, noting that the government alone cannot protect the integrity of Medicare and other federal health care programs.[18] Organizations are expected to police themselves and work with the government to correct problems. The OIG currently maintains a Provider Self-Disclosure Protocol on its Web site at http://www.oig.hhs.gov/authorities/docs/self-disclosure.pdf. Although not protected from civil or criminal action under the False Claims Act, providers disclosing fraud are advised in the Self-Disclosure Protocol that **self-reporting** of wrongdoing may offer mitigating factors. Also, by self-reporting, the provider may have the option of conducting a self-audit (following OIG guidelines) rather than an imposed government audit.

At a 1999 OIG/HCCA Government-Industry Roundtable, participants identified a series of questions to guide the scope of such an internal investigation (see "Building a Partnership for Effective Compliance: A Report on the Government-Industry Roundtable," April 2, 1999, available at *www.oig.hhs.gov/fraud/docs/complianeguidance/roundtale.htm*):

- **What is the origin of the issue?** A billing concern may be the result of a systematic practice, a third-party inquiry, or misconduct by individuals. A systematic noncompliant billing practice may have been tied to a new system implementation or the result of faulty advice received from a consultant or a Medicare contractor, for example.

- **When did the issue originate?** A systematic billing practice may warrant internal inquiry into the origin of the practice and the extent of its impact on the organization. Improper billing by one individual may require scrutiny of his or her entire employment history as well as a review of directions that person may have received from management.

- **How far back should the investigation go?** Investigation standards for one organization may not apply to another. Some providers will begin by reviewing the past one year's billing. Others may start with a month of prior billing. Some providers might designate a specific number of claims to be reviewed. Regardless of the methods used, the provider must determine the parameters of its investigation based on a reasonable approach that is justified under the circumstances.

- **Can extrapolation of a statistical sample be used?** Statistical sampling and extrapolation may be warranted when it is too difficult or costly to determine the exact cause of improper billing. Caution is warranted, however. Samples of improper billing may not accurately represent an organization's entire billing practices.

Understood, of course, is that any identified problem must be corrected immediately. Restitution of overpayments especially should be prompt. CMS regulations and contractor guidelines outline procedures for returning overpayments to the government. A provider should consult with its Medicare contractor for guidance regarding processing Medicare repayments and to establish the information necessary to quantify the amount of the overpayment. And when the problem is rectified, the issue should be added to the list of topics to be addressed with regular internal monitoring.

It is also possible that the government could approach the organization with information about an alleged violation—investigating a *qui tam* accusation, for example. In such an instance the government would conduct the internal investigation. If this happens, rumors and speculations will run rampant. It will be especially important to keep staff informed about what is going on. To get the message to employees, consider different ways of getting the message out. For example:

- The president or high-ranking administrator should send an all-staff memo or e-mail
- Hold an all-staff meeting to get the word out and answer questions
- Keep managers and department heads updated so they can "drill down" the message
- Provide opportunities for feedback and more questions from staff

Most important, the organization's policies and procedures should include instructions for employees on what to expect and how to handle contact from the government about an investigation. Legal counsel must be actively involved in the drafting of these policies. Search warrant policies and procedures should clearly identify who is responsible for fulfilling those procedures (usually the compliance officer). In the event of an on-site government investigation, legal counsel must be notified immediately, and to the extent possible, all nonessential employees should be sent home or relocated during the government search. The search warrant should be reviewed carefully to ensure only identified documents are searched. Also, the compliance officer should be present during the search, keeping a detailed, written account of all activities and an itemized inventory of documents inspected or removed from the premises. (See Appendix C, Responding to Search Warrants.)

CHAPTER 3

Organizational Steps

ORGANIZATIONAL STEPS

Gain Support and Commitment

Board of Directors or Board of Trustees Support

Compliance begins with the board of directors or board of trustees. Support from the top is very important; there can be no program at all, much less an effective one, without the vision and guidance of the board. It is the board that officially recognizes the need for a compliance program and authorizes its launch and implementation, including the hiring of a compliance officer. The Federal Sentencing Guidelines are very clear on the expected board commitment. The first step toward implementation of a compliance plan is management's communication of its commitment. A resolution or memo from the board stating its unequivocal support for the program is a strong beginning. The source of such a statement may be different depending on the organization. In some organizations it might come from the chairman of the board, in others from the CEO. A teaching hospital or medical school may want the statement to come from the dean. Whatever the source, board endorsement should be in a written format; it must communicate unqualified support for and commitment to the compliance process and ethical business behavior; and it must be effectively communicated to everyone.

One option is for the chairman of the board, CEO or the dean to distribute the memo or resolution to all department chairs. The department chairs then distribute the document to their managers so that the word trickles down and the message is reinforced that *all* managers endorse the compliance program. This approach also makes the compliance program directly accessible to staff and gives staff an opportunity to discuss the document in relatively small groups. A special department or unit meeting to discuss the program and distribute the letter can lend weight to the message. Or it can be an agenda item for a regularly scheduled meeting. Whatever the venue, staff should be given ample opportunity to ask questions and offer feedback.

Moreover, the board's role does not end with voting to establish a compliance program and distributing a letter of support—nor does its responsibility. Ongoing, visible support from the board of directors is crucial. Most people care about what the boss cares about. When the board takes compliance seriously, that sense of importance will trickle down. Your board may need guidance in understanding the seriousness of compliance. They may not immediately recognize that "doing the right thing" contributes to good business, that compliance is a good, long-term investment. The board of directors or board of trustees, meeting infrequently and not always aware of day-to-day operations, can be insulated from problems. But in the case of compliance, the board must understand the implications of not taking active measures to prevent potential wrongdoing. They should be educated about the potential for liability and reminded of the **Caremark International Derivative Litigation**, which makes the board responsible for implementation of a system to gather information on the company's efforts to prevent and detect fraud and abuse. It is in the best interest of the organization to have the board take an active rather than a passive role in compliance.

Management Support

Management plays an influencing role in making compliance work with support expressed in a myriad of ways. Attendance at educational programs cannot be mandatory for everyone except managers and vice presidents. Making time to demonstrate a personal commitment goes a long way to enhancing a system-wide commitment. After attending training sessions, managers should discuss the content with staff either at a regular department meeting or as circumstances permit.

Supervisors or managers must also lead by example, for actions speak louder than words. A manager cannot encourage employees to report questionable behavior and then give special treatment to a friend. And once a potential infraction is reported, the nonretaliation policy must be rigorously observed. It is up to management to make sure employees do not hesitate to come forward for fear of retaliation.

Staying on top of compliance issues is a manager's day-to-day obligation. Managers and supervisors must closely follow news and information from their professional organizations and pass along any and all compliance-related issues to the compliance office. The compliance officer is encouraged to be proactive and, from time to time, to ask managers and supervisors what new regulations are developing in their fields.

Physician Support

In the health care setting, the physician plays a key leadership role, so buy-in from physicians will be critical for any compliance program's success. There will be frequent situations when a physician's support can make all the difference. It will be to your advantage, therefore, to find a physician champion, someone who understands and supports the mission of the compliance program, someone who will back you up when you need it.

At the risk of generalization, physicians are, as a group, sometimes not enthusiastic about compliance. Physician buy-in has, in fact, been identified as among the top 10 obstacles to implementing an effective compliance program. If physicians seem skeptical, they may have good reason. Managed care has had a profound impact not just on remuneration but also on how medicine is practiced as well. And unless physicians understand what compliance means and how the program works, frustration will lead to opposition. But there are ways to communicate compliance to the physicians:[19]

- Discuss business and clinical aspects of an issue
- Emphasize clinical and fiscal improvements
- Build trust through involvement
- Involve physicians early in the process
- Give physicians lots of data
- Cultivate the early adopter and enthusiasts
- Be a partner, not a dictator
- Communicate, communicate, and communicate

The earlier you achieve physician buy-in the better. Invite physicians to compliance implementation committee meetings and actively seek their input throughout the start-up—and beyond. Many organizations have a strong physician presence on their compliance committees. If at all possible, consider having a physician chair the compliance committee. When funding permits, sending a key physician to a compliance conference can provide valuable education as well as increased awareness and facilitate support. Achieving physician buy-in will be an important challenge but it is a critical element of launching an effective compliance program.

Staff Support

It isn't a crime to make a mistake; it is a crime not to do anything about the mistake once it is detected. In launching a compliance program, staff will need to be convinced that looking for problem areas is not the sole responsibility of the compliance office—it is everyone's job. Education is the first step but also look for ways to heighten awareness on a day–to–day basis. When launching a compliance program, some organizations will distribute cups or pens with a compliance slogan and the organization name or logo. Everybody loves a freebie, and if the budget permits, these items can increase awareness and foster cooperation.

Staff buy-in will correlate directly with the organization's ability to foster an environment of trust. As emphasized earlier, accepting the nonretaliation policy as nothing short of gospel will be the best way to ensure active staff participation. Rewarding and thanking those who come forward to do the right thing will provide immediate positive feedback to staff and reap long–term rewards for the compliance program overall. The Federal Sentencing Guidelines suggests offering incentives to those who follow the compliance and ethics program.

Financial Support

Management up to and including the board of directors must also be willing to make a financial commitment to compliance. Remember, compliance is not cheap. Staffing and space cost money, and most health care organizations have limited, even diminishing resources. While the level of commitment is not necessarily correlated directly with the resources (human and financial) allocated, a reasonable budget must be developed in consultation with the compliance officer. An organization unwilling to commit the necessary resources isn't demonstrating support for the compliance program—and unquestionably and unfortunately—that message too will filter down through the organization.

Budget of Compliance Departments by Size of Organization

NUMBER OF EMPLOYEES

	All Respondents		Less Than 1,000		1,000 to 2,999		3,000 to 4,999		5,000 or More	
	#	%	#	%	#	%	#	%	#	%
Total Responses	587	100	210	100	173	100	74	100	117	100
Less than $100,000	147	25	97	46	40	23	5	7	3	3
$100,000 - $149,999	56	10	24	11	24	14	4	5	4	3
$150,000 - $299,999	101	17	26	12	40	23	22	30	11	9
$300,000 - $449,999	66	11	7	3	18	10	16	22	24	21
$450,000 - $599,999	44	7	6	3	18	10	6	8	14	12
$600,000 - $749,999	16	3	3	1	1	1	5	7	7	6
$750,000 - $899,999	14	2	1	0	2	1	4	5	7	6
$900,000 - $1,049,999	8	1	1	0	2	1	1	1	4	3
$1,050,000 - $1,299,999	12	2	0	0	3	2	2	3	5	4
$1,300,000 - $1,449,999	2	0	1	0	0	0	0	0	1	1
$1,450,000 +	22	4	1	0	0	0	1	1	20	17
Don't know	99	17	43	20	25	14	8	11	17	15

Compliance Budget

Knowing what to do won't make it happen. The reality is, you can't do it without money. But how much money? The right amount will depend on the organization, its size and scope. Remember, the compliance program must influence everyone in the organization; adequate funding will go a long way to demonstrating and eliciting commitment. This is a good place to mention again that the only thing worse than having no policies is having them and not following them. Underfunding can be one source of such a situation. If investigated, a compliance program's value in any settlement will depend largely on the government's interpretation of the organization's commitment to good corporate citizenship. In fact, "a compliance program that has neither the moral nor the budgetary support of senior management may actually be deemed as tacit approval for the inappropriate activities."[20]

Both external and internal risks and the controls to manage those risks factor into a budget. An identified risk area may require immediate attention and hence extra expense, perhaps specialized training or a new computer software program. Bear in mind that certain internal factors can impact, directly or indirectly, the compliance budget. For instance, if your organization has a high turnover rate, the compliance budget will need to provide for training the flow of new employees as well as the existing staff. A highly decentralized operation may call for either a centralization compliance process or additional monitoring to ensure procedures are consistent or at least consistently enforced. Other factors that can impact the compliance budget are poor communications infrastructure, poor data processing controls and compensation structures that emphasize financial performance with no compliance considerations.

Staffing

Organization size, setting, and culture will influence how the compliance department is staffed. In small organizations or physician practices the compliance officer role may not be full time, but rather a fraction of a full-time equivalent (FTE) position. In a large organization the compliance department will be much more extensive with a full-time compliance officer. According to aggregated data in the 2005 HCCA Profile of Health Care Compliance Officers, 66% of all responding organizations reported having two or more full-time employees in the compliance department.

For an organization able to consider more than one full-time employee, there are a variety of staffing possibilities. Because so much of compliance is education, an education coordinator can make a vital contribution to a program's effort. Other valuable positions include someone to accumulate and analyze compliance data and an auditor who can regularly review and help with documentation. Secretarial or administrative support may also be necessary.

For larger organizations considering staffing needs, it should be noted that every *facility or location* should have a compliance designate or compliance field liaison. A remote site clinic may not need a full-time compliance officer because the main site or hospital has such a position. But even "part-time" compliance personnel need appropriate training and resources, such as a binder of relevant information, on-site. Employees at the remote sites must be educated as well. Be sure to budget accordingly.

Ongoing Operations

There are other operational expenses to consider, beginning with some sort of reporting method. Hotlines can be handled internally or externally; the costs of each option will need to be assessed. Outsourcing may be more economically feasible for many organizations. When looking for outside help, secure competitive bids and be sure they are based on comparable information. It may be worthwhile to request outside proposals before you make a final decision. There's nothing to lose in finding out what outsourcing can do for you.

Educational materials can be a considerable compliance expense. There are several methods that can be utilized. Web-based training can be effective, especially in large organizations. There are many vendors who can help design a Web-based program for your organization. A video program produced by your organization for general sessions and new employee orientation can be helpful. Even so, a video customized to your organization can be very expensive, but there are "off the shelf" videos that may well meet your needs. You will also need to provide for specialized training for physicians as well as the coding and billing departments. Such training can be offered by a qualified internal individual, or can be provided through outside consultant specialists and hence will have budget implications. In-house and ongoing training may require audio-visual equipment and software to create engaging visual materials. There will be costs for printing announcements, agendas, and handouts. Costs for printing the code of conduct and policies and procedures can be a surprisingly large number. And while the code of conduct doesn't need to look like the annual report from a Fortune 500 company, this isn't a document to skimp on either. Find the right look and feel for your organization—just remember to budget accordingly.

Internet access today is a must. All relevant government documents are available online as are innumerable other helpful compliance-related sites. Adequate computer support is critical.

Professional journals and newsletters are vital ways of keeping abreast of new developments, **best practices**, and industry trends. They will also provide articles, suggestions and ideas that can be circulated to appropriate managers or adapted for internal newsletters. Consider budgeting each year for books so you can gradually build a compliance library that will be a resource for the compliance department, the compliance committee, and the organization. Also, membership in a professional organization such as the Health Care Compliance Association is a good investment. Belonging to a professional organization such as HCCA reinforces your professional standing and provides you with a growing network of invaluable resources.

Finally, if your organization has an in-house counsel, consult with him or her to determine budgetary needs. If you currently rely on external counsel, you may want to alert the firm of your new or expanding compliance program and solicit estimates for additional costs. Such expenses may be part of the legal budget but it is best to be sure they are appropriately covered somewhere.

Six Tips for Saving on Future Costs of Compliance[21]

1. **Embed quality into existing processes**—If processes that pose the greatest risk to the organization are revisited with an emphasis on quality, then the outcome of this exercise will be increased efficiency, increased customer satisfaction and better, less expensive compliance.

2. **Centralize common processes and controls**—Decentralized processes can lead to redundancy and inadequate oversight as well as extra expense.

3. **Improve human resources infrastructures**—Corporate culture is established by effective communication; communication is critical to training; training leads to compliance; compliance must be woven into the fabric of corporate culture. Turnover is the 'smart bomb' that disrupts the circle.

4. **Improve information system processes**—It is important and cost effective to embed compliance into technology through controls such as edit checks and reports that facilitate monitoring.

5. **Emphasize training**—The best way to correct an error is to prevent its occurrence.

6. **Monitor marketing and compensation**—Review marketing materials to be certain the message is consistent with corporate philosophy; new business ventures should be evaluated for risk and the ability of the organization to manage the risk; compensation structures should embed measurable compliance objectives.

Develop a Code of Conduct

When you roll out your compliance program to staff will depend on many factors. Certainly the sooner you can enlist staff participation the better. And you need not have everything absolutely final before you officially launch the compliance program companywide. However, you do need to have one of the most important foundation stones ready and in place as you begin: the organization code of conduct.

How the code of conduct is written can vary. In some organizations, it is prepared at the board of directors level. In others it is a compliance officer and/or compliance committee responsibility. If you are in the position of drafting your organization's code of conduct, there are many sources of sample materials. You can look for books with sample codes of conduct included. You could tap into your networking resources to solicit codes of conduct from other organizations. However, it is not advisable to "lift" a code of conduct from another source, make minor tweaks, and try to make it fit your organization. Your code of conduct should reflect your organization's spirit, tone, and culture. If it doesn't ring true to staff, securing their participation and cooperation in the compliance program will be much more difficult.

There may not be a "one size fits all" code of conduct but there are certain elements that every code should include. Most codes of conduct begin with the official board of trustees' or board of directors' resolution approving the compliance program or the memo announcing the launch of the program. The code should begin with this strong endorsement from the highest levels of management. An endorsement signed by the board chairman or the CEO makes the message personal and says "you have my word on it." This executive message is the place to state unequivocally that everyone in the organization and all affiliates are expected to act in an ethical manner and abide by all applicable laws and regulations affecting the organization. A strong message in support of staff is also in order. The code of conduct provides guidelines and tools developed to help employees in situations created by today's confusing and complex health care environment. Staff honesty is not the issue. When a situation poses uncertainty, the code of conduct provides guidance for appropriate conduct or, in more challenging situations, offers the way to get answers within the organization.

The code of conduct might be seen as an elaboration on the organization's mission or vision, both of which deserve a highly visible place in the code of conduct. Many organizations have identified specific values that help accomplish the mission. If your organization has values in addition to the mission, these too should be prominently featured in the code of conduct.

As a resource for all staff and affiliates, the code of conduct should also include a detailed outline of procedures for handling questions about compliance or ethical issues, beginning with a description of **chain of command**. The best reporting mechanism is an open door. When a question arises, it is hoped the employee will feel comfortable in approaching his or her supervisor, the first link in the chain of command. In the event that the employee and the supervisor cannot resolve the issue, usually the department manager is the next step. If discussions with the supervisor and department head are not satisfactory, in some organizations the corporate Human Resources representative is called in. Ultimately, if a compliance-related matter cannot be resolved at the department head or HR level, the corporate compliance officer, who represents executive management, gets involved. These steps should be delineated in the code of conduct along with a clearly stated promise of nonretaliation.

However, every employee will not be comfortable talking to management so there are alternate methods of reporting potential problems or posing questions.

The code of conduct should provide a clear, concise explanation of how those alternate reporting methods work. For instance, list the hotline (or helpline) telephone number along with hours of operation. In this context, emphasize that all calls will be anonymous or held in complete confidence. To the extent possible, it will help to outline the procedures for how the organization will respond to reports or questions. Can you promise that the compliance department will investigate all reports? Can you promise that all compliance-related questions or allegations, whether received through chain of command, the hotline, or other reporting mechanism, will be investigated within 48 hours? Such specifics are important to include but will be reassuring to staff only if they are achievable.

As a key element of an effective compliance program, every code of conduct will want to include a description of the compliance program along with names of all compliance office personnel and members of the compliance committee. Add phone numbers and e-mail addresses for all key contact personnel. The name of the board of director's compliance committee liaison and/or in-house corporate counsel may also be included, if appropriate.

The narrative section of the code of conduct can deal with a wide variety of issues, some of which may not be related to Medicare compliance specifically. For instance, policies on sexual harassment and controlled substances may be addressed. Every code will want to cover expectations regarding conflict of interest, acceptance of gifts and gratuities, Stark laws, and quality of care. Areas of specific weakness or risk should be addressed in the code, depending on the organizational setting. Most importantly, the code must emphasize zero tolerance for fraud or abuse, a commitment to submitting accurate and timely billing, and compliance with all laws and regulations. Consequences of malicious or uncorrected wrongdoing should be noted, with a description of the progressive discipline procedures, if appropriate. Also, clearly state that everyone has a personal obligation to report any possible wrongdoing. Not reporting makes an employee subject to discipline too.

The code of conduct holds the potential to be an abstract document, one that might not seem relevant to the day-to-day work of the individual. Therefore, many organizations add a "sample question" or "examples of compliance violations" section. A mixture of the general and specific is suggested. Sample general questions might be:

- I think I saw a violation of medical regulations. Who should I contact?
- Should I report a possible problem even if I'm not sure? Will I get in trouble?
- What if my supervisor asks me to do something I think is wrong?
- How can I be sure my report will be kept confidential?

Examples of compliance violations can be specific to your type of organization:

- To ensure Medicare payment, a billing department employee codes for services that are not reflected in the medical record.
- A physician or nurse asks someone else to make a chart notation.

Finally, most codes of conduct come with an acknowledgement or attestation form. The attestation form, requiring the employee signature, emphasizes the importance of the document and could provide certain legal advantages should there ever be a government inquiry. To encourage the employee to return the attestation form promptly, some organizations will require a signed attestation form before new employees can be assigned perquisites such as parking space. Attestation forms should be filed in the employee's official human resources file. The compliance department may want to maintain copies.

Identify Staffing Needs

The compliance officer, as noted earlier, is the "focal point" of the compliance program. Education and degree are important considerations in selecting a compliance officer, but more importantly, the position must be filled by someone who will be trusted and well respected within the organization. Background or experience must also be factored in. The compliance officer should have some background in health care administration. The HCCA 2005 Profile of Health Care Compliance Officer survey asked about the management level of the compliance officer and received these responses: 55% indicated the compliance officer was part of senior management, 26% indicated middle management, 15% indicated officer of the company and 4% identified another role.

All compliance department staff should have job descriptions. If need be, the compliance officer should develop his or her own job description. (See Appendix D, Sample Job Descriptions for Compliance Officers.) Job descriptions for additional department staff should include a detailed list of duties and responsibilities and, to the extent possible, measurable expectations. For an educational coordinator, for example, you might want to require an annual educational plan due by a specific date. An auditor might be expected to review a certain number of charts every month. Job descriptions may need to be modified and adapted as time goes by and as compliance requirements change. Regular employee input to the job description, perhaps in preparation for an annual performance review, will keep the document relevant.

Whatever the size and scope of the organization, all compliance department staff should have certain characteristics. The compliance department is an outreach department so good "people skills" are vital. There will also be daily interaction with a wide variety of personality types. The ability to stay unflappable will be an asset to someone working in compliance. Moreover, compliance has a lot to do with change and, in general, people don't like change. Therefore the compliance staff must, from time to time, be able to deal with unhappy, dissatisfied staff—especially when delivering difficult news that may mean more work. Strong communication and listening skills will be critical. Discretion is also required. A good sense of humor helps, too. As you interview, probe for these qualities. If you don't find them, keep looking at other candidates. Once you have hired, foster these qualities in your staff and provide feedback and guidance in performance reviews.

Most compliance officers would agree that a sizeable majority of compliance activities are related to education and training. Therefore, an education coordinator must be high on the list of early hires. As noted earlier, education is the first and best line of defense in compliance. An educated employee will be less likely to engage in an act of noncompliance and, knowing the organization's commitment to compliance, will be much more likely to come forward if there is a question or concern about potential noncompliance. Having someone to focus on education can make for more and effective educational programs and allow the compliance officer to coordinate the big picture. A training coordinator should have a strong background in health care and solid experience in adult learning strategies. Computer skills are needed not only for PowerPoint presentations but also for preparing and adapting handouts. Organizational skills are important; just keeping track of attendance can be a daunting task. Here, too, strong people skills are important.

Monitoring and auditing helps to ensure that the organization remains vigilant in its compliance efforts. Having someone on staff to coordinate these efforts will ensure that regular review happens and that it is objective, documented, reported, and analyzed. In this position, a background in health care and specifically experience with coding are mandatory. Consider a **certified professional coder** (Ex. CPC) for this position. A CPC monitoring coordinator in the compliance department could also work with the coding department and Human Resources to be sure competent coders are hired, especially today when hiring good people for any position seems to get harder and harder. For instance, consider administering a brief, simple test of perhaps 10 questions gleaned from the CPT4, HCPCS, and ICD9 books to coder applicants. Provide those books that would be available on the job and address basic coding questions. A candidate who cannot answer basic questions on such a test does not belong in the organization's coding or medical record auditing department. The first step toward prevention is to check competency up front. (Work closely with HR on any candidate testing to be sure requirements for administering the test consistently to all applicants is considered.)

Sample Coder Application Test Question

A physician's elderly female patient, who is residing in a rest home, requires a physician assessment for evaluation of chronic hypertension. The physician's assessment includes a problem-focused interval history, a problem-focused examination, and straight-forward medical decision making. "What is the code for the physician's services?" (Answer: 99331.)

The compliance committee composition is also an important staffing consideration. As noted earlier, the OIG encourages representation from a variety of departments within the organization, including operations, finance, auditing, human resources, utilization review, social work, discharge planning, medicine, coding and legal, as well as employees and managers of key operating units. To the extent you are able to influence the composition of the compliance committee, look for individuals who are respected leaders within the organization and who will be strong champions for compliance. Be sure there is good representation among physicians on the compliance committee (see Organizational Steps: Gain Support/Commitment, page 42).

The organization's legal counsel must work closely with the compliance department. Developing a solid working relationship between the two departments is critical. Communication should be open and frequent. To keep informed of ongoing compliance issues—and to identify any legal "red flags"—legal counsel should be an active member of the compliance committee. The compliance officer and legal counsel may want to meet regularly and separately from the compliance committee meetings. If in-house legal counsel is not available, outside counsel should be kept informed via regular written reports such as compliance committee minutes or periodic face-to-face meetings with verbal status reports.

Conduct Internal Assessment

One of the first steps in launching an effective compliance program is the **baseline audit**, or what the OIG calls a snapshot, of the operations from a compliance perspective. According to the OIG, this preliminary audit becomes the "baseline for the compliance officer and other managers to judge . . . progress in reducing or eliminating potential areas of vulnerability." Providing examples for hospitals, the OIG suggests that the baseline review "include the frequency and percentile levels of various diagnosis codes and the increased billing of complications and co-morbidities."[22] For third-party billing companies, the OIG suggests the baseline include "the frequency and percentile levels of CPT and HCPCS codes . . . and statistical data on claim rejection by code."[23]

The baseline audit has at least three main objectives. First, it *outlines the current operational standards* of the organization and the extent to which legal requirements are being met. Second, the baseline audit *identifies real and potential weaknesses,* especially for those procedures used to measure and enforce compliance with legal and regulatory requirements. Finally, it *offers recommendations* regarding necessary remedial action, areas of potential weakness to monitor closely, and targeted areas of need, among other things. These objectives combine to achieve the OIG stated goal of the baseline audit: "to facilitate identification of problem areas and elimination of potential areas of abusive or fraudulent conduct."[24] The baseline audit is distinct from subsequent audits, which evaluate the compliance program in operation or investigate an alleged violation. (See also Seven Elements: Monitoring and Auditing, page 28.)

In most organizations, the compliance officer cannot conduct such an extensive audit alone throughout the organization. The assistance and support of an executive-appointed baseline audit team are necessary. This team may be the core group that will ultimately grow into the compliance committee. Among its members, there should be experience and expertise in health care law, finance, and the organization's operations. (This does not preclude the contracting of outside health care specialists to conduct the baseline audit. Outside experts may offer greater objectivity and more health care compliance expertise than an internal team. Such a decision will depend on your organization's size and culture. The compliance officer must be actively involved in the baseline audit, even with outside specialists to provide the background and an understanding of the organization's operations.) The audit team first meets with senior management to outline or review the audit agenda or action plan, which will define the scope of the audit, identify types of documents to be reviewed, personnel to be interviewed, and a realistic timetable for completion. Executive management should consider informing staff of the audit, outlining its purpose and the expectation of cooperation, and also offering reassurances that the audit will have positive outcomes.

In drafting the audit agenda, it is important to manage the scope of the audit; otherwise it could easily become unwieldy and never-ending. The first place to start is by reviewing any previous problem areas. Those issues identified by the OIG in its various model compliance programs must be considered, but it is just as important to include individualized risk areas as well. Check for and review any previous audits, investigative reports, or evaluations such as Joint Commission survey reports. In addition, a look at existing policies will help determine any potential vulnerability. Are the policies and procedures appropriate? Are they being followed? A review of actual practices related to those procedures, as well as to government regulation, is also in order. It is important that the baseline audit should also analyze current education and training practices. Whatever the audit findings, staff will need to be educated on any changes resulting from the audit as well as implementation of the compliance program. If there is weakness in the education program, it must be addressed early on.

There are, of course, various government resources to help identify the audit agenda. The OIG Work Plan, *all* OIG model compliance guidance, OIG fraud alerts, and audit reports, among others, will be helpful. (The OIG Web site has all these resources and more: *www.oig.hhs.gov.*) Trade and professional associations also provide information on current issues and emerging trends, which can include potential risk areas for consideration in developing the baseline audit agenda.

There are two primary sources of information for the audit team: documents and staff. Begin by interviewing managers, those best acquainted with the organization's operations. This is also an excellent opportunity to personalize the compliance program. Open the discussion with information about yourself and plans for the compliance program. Be sure to explain the purpose of the interview and the audit and, if possible, mention what follow-up processes will be used. First, ask general questions and then move on to a more detailed level later. This is your opportunity to explore what is currently occurring and to identify the managers' areas of concern. Some sample topics for discussion:

- Functions and/or controls that are subject to frequent breakdowns
- The current compliance environment in the department
- The process for monitoring issues and how that information is reported
- How new regulations or policy changes are distributed
- How the department is trained on internal and external requirements
- How attendance records are maintained
- How the department's policies and procedures are developed and updated
- How is it verified that policies and procedures are being accurately implemented
- General methodology for communicating with direct reports

It is strongly advised that you take detailed notes during these interviews. A standardized form used by all baseline audit team members will ensure consistency. Ideally, a copy of the typed notes of each interview would be reviewed by the interviewee to ensure accuracy and secure buy-in.

As noted above, review of documentation should begin with an in-depth look at any previous audit reports or evaluations. Check carefully to see if recommendations were communicated to the appropriate parties and whether they were, in fact, implemented. In addition, all policies and procedures should be reviewed and checked for thoroughness and accuracy. Check, too, for availability of policies and procedures (do staff have ready access? do they know they have access?) and whether attestation forms have been secured and appropriately filed. Finally, it is important that training records be a part of the baseline audit in order to determine if education has been adequate and whether existing systems can handle implementation of a compliance program. Training information may need to be solicited from individual departments if there is no centralized system. Education plans, syllabi, handouts, and all attendance records should be reviewed and evaluated. Include information on outside education as well.

Once the audit is complete, the team will prepare a report for executive management. This report will identify any noncompliant standards and practices and make recommendations regarding remedial action. It is the starting point for developing the compliance program and it will serve as the "benchmark" to which future audits can be compared. Audit findings and all recommendations should be discussed with executive management prior to preparation of a final report to identify any unexplored issues or concerns. The goal is a complete, accurate, and realistic report that addresses the needs of the organization. The audit report has been compiled, in part, from interviews with managers, and they should receive a copy of the final report (along with a note of thanks) if at all possible. Keeping colleagues informed, even if the report content isn't all positive, will build trust and open lines of communications.

Develop Mission and Goals

Once the compliance staff is in place, it must function as a team toward a common goal. Building that sense of camaraderie within the compliance department is critical before you can begin building a compliance camaraderie throughout the organization. One way to build that camaraderie is to conduct an annual retreat for the compliance personnel. As always, the size and setting of the organization as well as logistical issues must be considered. But when possible, an off-site retreat can be invigorating, motivating, and enormously productive. Off-site sessions are preferred only to eliminate, or at least minimize, the distractions of telephone calls, meetings, and "quick questions" from staff. The first retreat should be dedicated to drafting a mission statement for the department, a mission statement consistent with the organization's mission statement. It is important for everyone in the compliance department "to understand that fit and to be reading from the same page."

Sample Compliance Department Mission Statement
Courtesy of the Office of Compliance, University of Louisville Health Sciences Center

To strive to provide the highest quality of education and monitoring to assure integrity in the ethical and legal aspects of medical billing compliance for the University of Louisville Health Sciences Center and promote community awareness.

The retreat agenda should also look at goals for the upcoming year (which need not be a calendar year) and review progress toward current year goals. Be sure to identify a realistic number of goals and assure that they are achievable and measurable. Not all goals will be measured quantitatively. But when discussing goals at the retreat, explore with staff how success will be measured. Goals need not be directly tied to specific problems, but the retreat does provide an opportunity for staff to discuss openly any problems or concerns.

Sample Compliance Department Annual Goals

- To provide a positive compliance experience.
- To develop and maintain clear lines of communication with key personnel throughout the university.
- To provide diverse educational opportunities to meet the demands of the School of Medicine and its community.
- To provide a compliance Web site.
- To create and provide quality resources that will optimize compliance activity within the medical community.
- To establish a compliance reference library.
- To promote the Health Care Compliance Professional's Code of Ethics.
- To elevate awareness and increase participation regarding compliance issues throughout the medical community.
- To expand the collaborative relationships with regional academic compliance professionals.
- To maintain an open-door policy fostering confidentiality and trustworthiness.

The more active a role that staff takes in developing the mission statement, especially the goals, the more they will feel "ownership" of them and the more likely they will be to succeed.

However goals are determined, it is important that they be effectively and regularly communicated to the department staff. Discussing and measuring progress along the way, with updates at regular staff meetings, will contribute significantly toward progress. Assigning a department "liaison" for each goal can also contribute to ownership and stimulate progress. A department retreat will help communicate goals to staff. However, should any goals come to the department from executive management, these should be communicated and incorporated into tracking and measuring practices.

Consider doing an annual compliance report. The compliance department will provide a detailed annual compliance status report to the board of directors or the board of trustees and the organization's executive management. An annual report is a different document, one meant for the board as well as all staff. The Compliance Annual Report is an opportunity to communicate your mission and goals to the organization. It is also an opportunity to talk about the organization's compliance success stories, thereby reinforcing positive images of compliance and fostering support. Thanking compliance champions, and those who came forward to identify problems, provides positive reinforcement throughout the organization. The all-staff Compliance Annual Report need not be glitzy and expensive. The point is to get the word out and to build support. Use the data that you've gathered and show your enthusiasm. It can be contagious. The University of Louisville's Annual Report can be found as an example at *www.louisville.edu/medschool/compliance.*

P-D-C-A

Once a compliance program is up and running, it needs the "care and feeding" of ongoing evaluation. Getting a handle on regular review can be difficult, indeed it can be as daunting as getting started. For this process, consider the PDCA approach: Plan—Do—Check—Act, a tried and true quality management technique. (For more information on the PDCA cycle, see *The Team Handbook: How to Use Teams to Improve Quality* by P. R. Scholtes. Madison, WI. Joiner Associates Inc. 1988.)

- **Plan**—Look to your compliance program. Meet with the compliance committee to discuss and document current position and possible next steps.
- **Do**—Take baby steps. Make preliminary attempts at next steps with full knowledge that there may be some false steps along the way.
- **Check**—Review lessons learned. Gather the take-home lessons for those preliminary attempts.
- **Act**—With your compliance committee, decide how to incorporate what you've learned with what you still need to do.

Compliance is an ongoing process. PDCA can keep it flowing.

CHAPTER 4

Tailoring Your Compliance Program

TAILORING YOUR COMPLIANCE PROGRAM

The compliance program must be tailored to fit your organization. There is not a "one size fits all" program. As we have discussed, you need commitment from the top that supports your program, financial support including necessary staffing, and a continual assessment of your program. Once you understand the organization's needs, then fit your plan to the organization. The code of conduct should be the focal point of your program.

Communication

Communication of your program's expectations and goals is a key to its success. The communication must be clear, concise, and creative. Much of compliance-related information can be difficult to understand because so much of it is buried in thousands of pages of government regulations. The written standards of conduct and policies and procedures should be clear and easy to understand and distributed to all staff. What good is the compliance plan if no one in the organization knows it exists? Compliance may not be an exciting topic for everyone, so be creative and use many methods to communicate. Be creative and keep your program fresh and exciting.

The 3 Cs of Communication

- Clear
- Concise
- Creative

There are many ways to communicate the compliance message. Communicating can include walking rounds with the providers, one-on-one training, skits at staff meetings, or role-play exercises during education sessions. Look for ways your organization celebrates successes and tap into them. If your organization has a holiday party, consider contributing in some visible and fun way, a skit or karaoke song for example, if that fits your organization's culture. Items with a compliance theme or message can be popular, assuming the budget allows. Magnets or pens can be inexpensive enough to allow distribution to all employees. Posters, brochures, and wallet cards can also be effective. Consider a compliance open house or a "road show" to other departments. Your reporting system is also a communication tool. Make sure all employees know about the hotline or other systems you have in place. And as much as is possible, get back to them with results—results of investigating hotline questions, results of compliance successes, results of audits. The most important communication device is an open-door policy in the compliance department. Help managers to be open to employee questions. Encourage all staff to stop by the compliance office with questions or concerns. The accessibility of the compliance officer will communicate much more than the specifics of regulations and laws; it will communicate a sense of mutual trust and common goals.

Continual Evaluation

You have your plan. And you have communicated it to all staff. Now what do you do with it? The compliance plan should be reviewed at least annually. There may be a new regulation or law, new guidelines from the OIG. Changes will need to be made. Ask yourself if what you have in writing is really occurring. Is it working? Could it be improved? The compliance oversight committee should take an active role in this process.

In addition, all policies and procedures need to be monitored. A complete review of each policy should be done at least annually. Such a task can obviously become overwhelming, so you may want to consider a predetermined schedule for reviewing policies and procedures. Certain policies can be reviewed in January, for example, another batch in April and so on. Here, too, the compliance committee can be of help. As you look at the policies and procedures, consider if they are still necessary. It's possible a new policy has superceded an existing one. Have circumstances changed to warrant revising a policy or procedure? Are the policies and procedures effective? And as we have discussed, policies that are written and not followed can lead to trouble. Be sure to evaluate whether all employees are aware of the policies and procedures pertinent to their positions. You can't expect them to follow policies if they don't know about them.

Benchmarking against yourself is also a good way to measure and evaluate your program. Your annual report provides one regular statistical summation that can be used to develop benchmarking statistics. You might track and compare the number of educational programs delivered or the number of employees trained in a given period, for example. Or compare number of claims filed and percentage of claims approved (a more positive slant than percentage declined). Just be sure you collect consistent data so comparisons of results are viable.

Evaluating for Success

- Annual review of written compliance program
- Continual review of individual policies and procedures
- Benchmarking against your own statistics

Measuring Effectiveness

The OIG guidance frequently refers to the "effective compliance program." How can you tell if your program is effective? What is effectiveness? It has not been defined in exact words but, in general, if the program includes the seven elements and the program is active and making a difference, that can be considered effectiveness.

Effectiveness Measures

As identified by Compliance 101 educational seminar participants

- Staff knowledge
- All seven elements included in the program
- Comparing issues year to year
- Tracking and trending complaints
- Tracking corrective actions
- Reviewing concurrent audits
- Educational session pre- and post-tests
- Tracking "bill denials"
- Organizational survey results
- Audit results
- Compliance topics on department/organization agendas

But how do you get there? One method, outlined by William Altman in the *Journal of Health Care Compliance*, identifies three measures of effectiveness: structure, process, and outcome. Structure refers to the capacity of a health care organization to provide care, including staffing levels and policies and procedures. Process refers to performance measures or the manner in which care is delivered. And outcome addresses observable, measurable results of care or clinical indicators. Altman concludes that "the context of compliance program effectiveness should be clearly understood before reaching conclusions about the effectiveness of any given program." That *context* is critical. Different measures may be required for annual evaluation than those required for an identified improvement.

Six Steps to Building a Framework for Effectiveness[25]

1. Identify compliance risk areas

2. Identify how the organization addresses the identified risk areas by categorizing compliance program elements into structure, process and outcome measures

3. Assess the "maturity" of the compliance program before drawing definitive conclusions about effectiveness

4. Evaluate the extent to which structure, process and outcome measures of effectiveness are viewed as "linked" by the compliance program

5. Evaluate the extent to which the compliance program is "dynamic" and continuously changes in response to internal and external factors

6. Measure compliance program effectiveness against both government and organizational goals

Organizational Fit

The importance and value of the code of conduct cannot be emphasized enough. The code of conduct must address your organization's culture, its beliefs, and its ethical position. The code of conduct—and the compliance program—must understand, accept, and "live" the organization's mission, vision, and objectives. Your code of conduct may include photographs of staff. It may have sample questions and sample situations specific to the scope and setting of your organization. It may be distributed at an all-staff meeting with a speech from the chairman of the board. Or it might be distributed by individual managers at a regular department meeting. You must be sensitive to your organizational needs and incorporate compliance in ways that will be consistent with the existing way of doing things. Culture will drive your program. While there may be things you want to change, remember that change can be difficult for many people. To the extent you can keep it familiar, your job will be a bit easier.

Advancing Your Program

A compliance program is never finished; it should always be a work in progress. You must work to expand your program to fit the needs of your organization. Never be satisfied with the status quo. Look at the big picture. Many programs began with coding and billing compliance, but have evolved into other areas, such as research, and HIPAA. Organizations need to stay abreast of changes, new laws and regulations and assure that the program expands to encompass all these changes and newly identified risks. The compliance officer needs to constantly be on the lookout for ways to enhance and broaden the compliance program.

Change

If a compliance program is never finished, if it is a work in progress, then change will be the one sure constant in the compliance officer's job. Merriam-Webster's dictionary gives several meanings for the word *change*. One is "to make different." Among six other definitions are "to undergo a modification" and "to transform." The dictionary doesn't say anything about how difficult change can be. But for many, change can be very frustrating. Just when you think you have it, it changes. We all know that feeling. But that is what compliance is all about. Death, taxes, and changes in compliance guidelines and regulations—all sure things. But that's also what makes compliance one of the most exciting fields in health care today. With change comes new challenges. You will be challenged constantly to remain abreast of new regulations, to sense the pulse of the industry, to learn innovative ways to motivate and educate staff, to find new strategies to keep executive management informed and involved—in short, challenged always to stay at the top of your game. The work isn't necessarily easy—but it is important. Through change you can make a difference.

CHAPTER 5

Health Insurance Portability and Accountability Act

by Marti Arvin

Health Insurance Portability and Accountability Act

The Health Insurance Portability and Accountability Act (HIPAA) was passed in 1996. HIPAA incorporates several legislative actions. The legislative actions include the availability, portability and renewability of health insurance; changes to fraud and abuse laws; the Administrative Simplification Section; tax provisions; application and enforcement provisions of group **health plan** regulations and revenue offsets. The **Administrative Simplification Section of Title II** is the section that triggered the regulations for standard transactions and code sets, privacy and security of health information, and unique health identifiers.

HIPAA changed the way health information is shared among the players in the health care market. What was once governed by individual state laws is now a federal law and corresponding regulations.

Most health care providers are impacted by the Administrative Simplification Section of HIPAA in virtually every aspect of their work. This chapter will discuss the three primary regulations under this section of HIPAA. Before discussing the specifics of these three sections, it may be helpful to understand why HIPAA includes a section titled "Administrative Simplification."

Background

Congress recognized approximately 24 cents of every dollar spent on health care was being spent on administrative costs and not on what was most important: the provision of health care to individuals. One reason for the high administrative costs was the use of proprietary transactions between those who provided health care and those who paid for health care. Congress identified more than 400 proprietary methods for transmitting information between providers and payors. The solution was to mandate standard formats for transactions and code sets used in health care.

The standardization of electronic health information brought with it an increased concern that **health information** could be more readily used or acquired for inappropriate purposes. As a result, Congress added the provisions to the statute that paved the way for what are now commonly referred to as the HIPAA privacy and security regulations. With this brief background, the three primary regulatory provisions can now be addressed. Any piece of legislation passed by Congress will result in new terms and acronyms. HIPAA is no exception. Key terms are included in the glossary. Review of these terms may be necessary to better understand concepts discussed in this chapter.

What does HIPAA govern and who must comply with these new regulations?
HIPAA governs the **use** and **disclosure** of **protected health information (PHI)** by **"covered entities"** directly and their **business associates** indirectly. If the organization in question does not fit the definition of a covered entity, the regulations do not apply.

Standard Transactions and Code Sets

The technical make-up of a standard transaction is beyond the introductory intent of this chapter. However, an introduction to the standard transactions and code sets is appropriate. The standard transactions under HIPAA are:

837 – Claims/Encounter
834 – Enrollment/Disenrollment
270, 271 – Eligibility
835 – Payment and remittance advice
811, 820 – Premium Payments
276, 277 – Claims Status
278 – Referral Certification and authorization
The standard code sets under HIPAA are:
ICD-9-CM
HCPCS Level I codes (CPT ® codes)
HCPCS Level II codes (medical and surgical supplies)
CDT
NDC

Being able to communicate in one standardized methodology will ultimately reduce the administrative cost of health care. This will allow the health care industry to use dollars previously spent on administrative costs to pay for the provision of health care.

HIPAA Privacy Regulations

Keeping patient information confidential is not a new concept to health care providers. It has always been part of the ethical obligations of the physician-patient relationship. However, an overriding theme to the privacy regulations is to place control over health information squarely in the hands of the individual who is the subject of the information. Thus, in addition to regulating the uses and disclosures of protected health information (PHI) held by a covered entity, the privacy regulations also provide individuals with certain rights regarding their PHI.

The privacy regulations were drafted with the intent of allowing the free flow of information for the provision of health care and for other purposes in the public interest. If a covered entity is not using or disclosing PHI for the direct provision of health care and related activities, then the method by which the information can be used, accessed, or disclosed will be limited.

The privacy regulations can be broken down into two major categories: ways in which PHI can be used or disclosed, and the rights provided to individuals regarding their PHI. The ways that PHI can be used or disclosed can be further divided into three subcategories:

1. Uses and disclosures without an individual's explicit permission

2. Permitted uses and disclosures if the covered entity has given the individual an opportunity to object

3. Uses and disclosures only with the individual's explicit permission

Access for Treatment, Payment and Health Care Operations

The first way to access PHI is when the use or disclosure is intended for **treatment**, **payment**, or **health care operations**. If the use or disclosure of the PHI fits into one of these three definitions, the PHI can be used or disclosed without getting explicit permission from the individual. This allowance ties directly to the intent of the privacy regulations to allow for the free flow of PHI for purposes directly related to the provision of health care. Requiring an individual's permission to use or disclose PHI for these purposes, commonly referred to as TPO, was deemed too cumbersome to allow for efficient and effective delivery of health care.

Examples of TPO uses or disclosures:

Treatment—A physician can call his or her colleague in another specialty to get the colleague's input on the care being provided.

Payment—A physician's staff can submit a bill to the individual's insurance company to obtain payment for the service provided.

Health Care Operations—A physician's compliance staff can access the individual's PHI to conduct an assessment of the physician's coding and documentation practices.

Access for Purposes in the Public Interest

There is a second way to access PHI. This access is permitted when the use or disclosure is deemed to be in the public interest. Most of the uses and disclosures under these provisions carry restrictions on the circumstances under which the PHI can be used or disclosed and to whom it can be disclosed. It is important to understand that the privacy regulations permit, but do not require, the covered entity to use or disclose PHI for purposes in the public interest.

There are only two instances under the privacy regulations when the covered entity is required to disclose PHI: when the information is requested by a Secretary of the Department of Health and Human Services to investigate an allegation of a privacy violation, and when the subject of the information requests it. There are some restrictions on what PHI the individual is entitled to receive. These restrictions are discussed in detail under the section on the individual's right to access and copy PHI.

There are eleven categories under which a covered entity is permitted to disclose information in the public interest without first obtaining the individual's explicit permission. The categories include:

- public health activities
- reporting on victims of abuse, neglect or domestic violence
- reporting for health oversight activities
- judicial or administrative proceedings
- law enforcement purposes
- information to coroners, medical examiners, and funeral directors about decedents
- information for organ donation
- certain research purposes
- disclosures to avert a serious threat to health or safety
- specialized governmental functions
- workers' compensation

The details regarding circumstances when PHI can be used or disclosed for the listed public interest purposes are quite extensive. State law may also have a significant impact on uses and disclosures in the public interest. A discussion of these provisions with someone familiar with the particulars of the specific state or region where one practices is recommended.

Access Requiring an Opportunity to Object

The group of circumstances for which a use or disclosure of PHI is permitted without first obtaining the individual's explicit permission require that the individual be given an opportunity to object. Any one of the three purposes will allow access to the PHI.

The first purpose is when a covered entity includes limited information about the individual in its facility directory. An individual's name, location within the covered entity, general condition, and religious affiliation may be maintained in a directory. The information may be shared with members of the clergy. Other individuals inquiring about the individual by name can get the person's name, location, and general condition. The subject of the PHI must be informed of the information that will be included in the directory and given an opportunity to object to the inclusion of all or some of her PHI in the directory. The individual must also be allowed to restrict to whom the directory information is disclosed. For example, an individual might not object to information being included in the directory, but may not want it disclosed to a clergy member asking for information about individuals with a certain religious affiliation.

A second disclosure can be made if the individual is given an opportunity to object. In this situation, a disclosure can be made to family, friends, or others involved in the individual's care or payment for the care. The information disclosed must be directly related to the individual's involvement in the subject's care. When the subject of the PHI is present, the disclosure can be made if the individual agrees to the disclosure, if the individual does not object to the disclosure, or if under the circumstances, one can reasonably infer in the exercise of professional judgment that the individual does not object.

If the individual is not present or is incapacitated, a disclosure to family, friends, or others involved in the individual's care may be made if, in the exercise of professional judgment, the disclosure is in the best interest of the individual, and the disclosure is limited to the PHI relevant to the party's involvement in the individual's care.

Finally, a covered entity can disclose PHI under this provision for purposes of assisting in disaster relief. The disclosure can be made to either a private or public entity authorized by law, or by its character, to assist with disaster relief. Such disclosures would generally be made so the location and condition of the individual could be accessible to family and friends.

All Other Uses and Disclosures of PHI

The fourth and final way to access PHI is an authorization. An authorization is the document used to get an individual's permission to access PHI for a particular use or disclosure. An authorization must be used if the intended use or disclosure of PHI does not fit one of the categories already discussed.

An authorization is valid only if it contains the required elements as defined by the privacy regulation. An authorization must contain:

- Description of the PHI to be used or disclosed in a specific and meaningful fashion

- Name or other specific identification of the person or class of person(s) authorized to make the use or disclosure of the PHI

- Name or other specific identification of the person or class of person(s) authorized to receive the PHI

- Description of the purpose of each requested use or disclosure

- An expiration date

- Signature of the individual and date

- Statement informing the individual of the right to revoke the authorization in writing

- Any restrictions on the individual's right to revoke and instructions for how the authorization can be revoked

- A statement informing the individual that signing the authorization is a pre-condition of treatment, participation in research, eligibility for benefits, or enrollment in a health plan, if applicable.

- Statement informing the individual that the recipient of the PHI may re-disclose it in a manner that makes it no longer protected by the privacy regulations

The individual is entitled to a copy of the authorization. If an authorization does not include all the required elements, it is not valid and a covered entity cannot rely on it to use or disclose PHI. Marketing and fundraising are just two examples of uses and disclosures that require an authorization. As with any rule, however, there are exceptions. If a covered entity wants to engage in fundraising, the HIPAA privacy rule permits the use of the limited PHI without an authorization. The limited PHI includes demographic information such as name, address, or other contact information, insurance status and date of care. This information can be used for fundraising by the covered entity or it can be disclosed to the covered entities business associate or an institutionally related foundation. If the covered entity wants to use additional PHI, an authorization from the individual would be required. Marketing activities also have an exception.

If the marketing activity is done in a face-to-face encounter with the individual, or if an item of nominal value is given to the individual, an authorization is not required. For all other marketing activities, an authorization is required. It is helpful to note that the definition of marketing under HIPAA does not include information given to an individual about particular benefits or service that is part of her health plan; information related to the treatment of the individual or information about alternative treatments, therapies, health care providers or settings of care.

Individual Rights Under the Privacy Rule

The federal privacy regulations under HIPAA granted individuals certain rights to be informed about and to control their PHI. Individuals were given the right to access and copy PHI, request an amendment to PHI, receive an accounting of disclosures of their PHI, receive a notice of privacy practices, request restrictions on certain uses and disclosures of their PHI, and request to have communications about their PHI conducted in a confidential manner.

While each of these rights appears on the surface to be straightforward, some additional discussion is warranted. It is important that covered entities fully understand the exact nature of each right that HIPAA grants individuals.

Right to Access and Inspect

The right of individuals to access and inspect their records, granted by HIPAA, is not unfettered. Individuals cannot necessarily have access to everything in the record. The covered entity can restrict the individual's access to such things as psychotherapy notes; information the covered entity compiled to prepare for actual or anticipated litigation; or PHI that the covered entity is prohibited from sharing pursuant to the Clinical Laboratory Improvements Amendments of 1988. A covered entity that is a correctional institution may also restrict an inmate's access to his PHI if the access would put the security of the individual, another inmate, or the institution at risk. Finally the PHI can be restricted from an individual's access if the PHI was obtained during a research study and the individual agreed to the restricted access in the authorization signed at the beginning of the study; if the PHI was obtained from someone other than a health care provider and the individual was promised confidentiality; or the PHI is subject to the federal Privacy Act.

A covered entity may also deny an individual access to PHI if a licensed health care professional has determined, based on her professional judgment, any of the following:

- Sharing the information would put the individual or another person in danger

- The information was obtained from someone other than another health care provider and sharing the information would be reasonably likely to put that person at risk for substantial harm

- The request for access is by a personal representative and sharing the information would be reasonably likely to put the subject of the information or another person at substantial risk of harm

If the individual is denied access for any of these three reasons, the covered entity is required to provide a method for the individual to appeal the denial. Another licensed health care professional must review the decision. The licensed health care professional reviewing the denial must not have been involved in the original decision to deny access. The covered entity is required to abide by the decision of the reviewing official.

Right to an Amendment of PHI

An individual may believe certain information in their health record is inaccurate or incomplete. Under HIPAA the individual may ask to have the record amended to correct the inaccurate or incomplete information. If the information is found to be inaccurate or incomplete, the covered entity may correct the record in a manner consistent with the entity's policies and procedures. Note that as a general rule, original information documented in a medical record should not be altered in such a way as to completely eliminate the information.

A covered entity is not always required to make the requested amendment to the record. If the covered entity has determined that the record is accurate and complete, the individual's request for the amendment may be denied. The covered entity may also deny requests for other reasons. One reason is that the information was not generated by the covered entity. Another reason is that the individual wishes to amend information that he or she is not entitled to access, or that the information is not part of the **designated record set**.

Right to Request Restrictions and Confidential Communications

An individual may request additional restrictions on the uses and disclosures of PHI when the use or disclosure is for treatment, payment or health care operations, or the disclosure is to a family member, friend or another individual involved in the patient's care or payment for the care. These are the only uses and disclosures that the individual is allowed to further restrict.

The privacy rule is very explicit. While an individual has the right to request a restriction, the covered entity is under no obligation to agree to the restriction. If a covered entity does agree to the additional restriction on the use or disclosure of PHI, then the covered entity is bound by its agreement. Generally, the administrative burden of monitoring such restrictions for a covered entity of any significant size makes agreeing to the restrictions overly burdensome.

Unlike restrictions which further limit the manner in which PHI can be used or disclosed, a request for a confidential communication addresses the manner in which PHI is communicated. If an individual makes a reasonable request to have PHI communicated in a specific manner, a health care provider is required to accommodate the request. What does this mean? An individual may ask that the provider only call one number to communicate PHI. The individual may ask that no messages are left on an answering machine or that messages are left only on the voicemail of the individual's cell phone. Unless the provider has a basis for arguing that the individual's request is unreasonable, an accommodation must be made to meet the request.

The confidential communication rule varies slightly for health plans. If a health plan receives a reasonable request for a confidential communication, accommodation of the request can be contingent on the individual stating that disclosure of the information in another manner could endanger the individual.

Right to Request an Accounting of Disclosures

The HIPAA privacy regulations give an individual the right to know who has received his or her PHI. If an individual requests an accounting of disclosures, a covered entity must be prepared to provide the individual with a list of all the disclosures it has made of the individual's PHI. The good news is that not every disclosure requires an accounting. An accounting is not required if the disclosure was:

- For TPO
- An incidental disclosure
- Made in a limited data set
- Made with an authorization from the individual
- Made for national security purposes
- A disclosure prior to the enforcement date of the privacy regulations, April 14, 2003
- A disclosure to the subject of the information
- A disclosure that only required giving the individual an opportunity to object
- A disclosure to a correctional institution or other law enforcement official having custody of the individual for purposes of providing appropriate care to the individual

The accounting must include: who received the information, the date the disclosure was made, a brief description of the information disclosed, and a brief statement of the purpose of the disclosure. An individual may request an accounting that covers up to a six-year period. However, keep in mind that the six-year period cannot go any further into the past than April 14, 2003.

Right to a Notice of Privacy Practices

The privacy regulations require that covered health care providers and health plans provide individuals with a notice of their privacy practices. The notice lets the individual know how the covered entity will use and disclose PHI, what the covered entity's legal obligations are under HIPAA, and what the individual's rights are under HIPAA. The notice should be carefully drafted. A covered entity is bound by the notice. Thus, if the notice does not fully describe how PHI is used and disclosed, it could be argued that the covered entity's ability to use and disclose information is more restrictive than what the privacy regulations allow.

The notice must be provided to the individual at the first episode of care. The covered entity is required to make a good faith effort to obtain an acknowledgement from the individual that the notice of privacy practices was received. If the first episode of care was via the telephone, the covered entity must mail its notice to the individual within 24 hours. Calling the physician's office to schedule an appointment, or calling the hospital to schedule a procedure, would not be considered an episode of care.

Other issues under the HIPAA privacy rule

The ways PHI can be used and disclosed under the HIPAA privacy regulations and the rights the regulations grant to an individual have been discussed. There remain some overriding principles of the HIPAA privacy regulations that need to be discussed.

The concepts include terms that may be new to many health care professionals: terms like minimal necessary, verification, need-to-know and business associate. In addition, HIPAA creates some new organizational arrangements that warrant a brief discussion.

The term *minimal necessary* is used in HIPAA to identify the amount of PHI that can be used or disclosed in a particular circumstance. For most uses and disclosures of PHI, the regulation requires that the covered entity only share the minimal amount actually needed to accomplish the task or activity. Virtually any time a covered entity makes a use or disclosure, an evaluation of minimal necessary will be required. There are certain circumstances under which a minimal necessary evaluation is not required. These are uses or disclosures made:

- With an authorization
- To a provider for treatment
- To the subject of the information
- To the Secretary of DHHS
- As required by law
- As required to comply with the regulations

What constitutes the minimal amount necessary will be based on the situation. However, if a covered entity makes routine uses or disclosures for particular purposes, a policy and procedure can be written to define minimal necessary. This eliminates the need to evaluate each use or disclosure.

Minimal necessary also ties to two additional concepts: role based access and need-to-know. Role based access means only allowing employees and others access to the information that is needed to perform their role in the organization. For example, a nurse in the ICU may need a different level of access than a dietician.

The second concept, need-to-know, is generally an educational process. There may be instances where a covered entity grants an individual full access to the medical record because it is appropriate based on her role. However, it is unlikely the individual will have a business need-to-know for all the information she has the ability to access. For example, a physician or resident may be granted access to the entire electronic medical record of a covered entity. If the physician does not have a treatment relationship with a particular patient, it would not be appropriate for her to look at the record. Stated another way, the ability to access PHI does not mean that there is a need-to-know the information.

Covered entities must determine the appropriate level of access to be granted to various individuals based on their role. The next step is to educate those individuals regarding the proper uses and disclosures of the PHI to which they have been given access.

Verification

When PHI is requested from a covered entity, how does the covered entity know that the party making the request is legitimately entitled to the PHI being requested? There is not a definitive answer to this question. However, the privacy regulations do require the covered entity to have in place reasonable methods to verify that the individual is who she says she is, and that she has the right to receive the information.

For example: If a physician calls the hospital requesting lab results, the hospital staff could ask a few questions to verify the physician has a treatment relationship to the individual whose information is being requested. The physician might be asked for DOB, MRN, the reason for the lab test, or some other piece of information.

There is no magic formula to determine what is reasonable. Most important is that a covered entity has a process for verification, a rationale for why the process is reasonable, and evidence that the process is consistently followed.

The HIPAA privacy regulations also introduced three new terms related to business arrangements. The three arrangements are as follows:

- Organized Health Care Arrangements (OHCA)

- Affiliated Covered Entities (ACE)
- Hybrid Covered Entities (HCE)

An organized health care arrangement or OHCA is a clinically integrated setting where the individual typically receives health care from more than one health care provider. An example of this might be a hospital and its medical staff. The hospital is one covered entity. The physicians who make up the medical staff might be from one or multiple covered entities. Agreeing to participate in an OHCA allows the covered entities to have a joint notice. The notice covers the manner in which all members of the OHCA will use and disclose PHI about the individual. An OHCA also allows the participants to share PHI for health care operations. Without an OHCA there are limitations on the PHI that can be shared among covered entities for health care operations. If a physician participates in an OHCA and agrees to the joint notice, it is important to understand that the notice only applies to services provided within the OHCA. This means that the physician must still distribute a notice to the patients seen in a private practice clinic.

Another arrangement HIPAA defines is an affiliated covered entity or ACE. An ACE is a group of legally separate covered entities that share common ownership or control. Common ownership exists if an entity or entities possess five percent or greater ownership interest in another entity. Common control exists if one covered entity has the ability to significantly influence the actions or policies and procedures of another covered entity, either directly or indirectly. Common ownership is relatively easy to determine. What constitutes sufficient ability to influence the actions or policies and procedures is a question that can only be answered based on the facts of each situation.

An ACE allows a group of covered entities to function as one covered entity for most purposes under HIPAA. However, the designation as an ACE does not make all the legally separate entities liable for privacy violations of the other members.

Finally, a covered entity may wish to designate itself as an HCE. An HCE is a business that has, as one of its functions, an activity or activities that make it a health care provider, a health plan and/or a **health care clearinghouse**. Under the privacy regulations, the entire business would be a covered entity and subject to the regulations. However, the business is given the option to designate itself as an HCE. The components of the business that engage in HIPAA covered functions are designated as the covered component and the remaining portions are designated as the non-covered portion. The covered component is required to include those segments that would not be covered entities but, if legally separate from the remainder of the covered entity, would be engaged in business associate type activities.

Business Associates

These are the people such as accountants, outside legal counsel, transcription agencies, billing, and other vendors with whom a covered entity conducts business on a day-to-day basis. Before PHI can be shared between a covered entity and a business associate, the business associate must provide satisfactory assurances that it will not use or disclose protected health information (PHI), in a manner that contradicts the Privacy Rule requirements. The regulation also requires a business associate agreement that defines the function of the business associate and the limitations on their uses and disclosures of PHI. The business associate agreement must also define what will happen to the PHI held by the business associate upon termination of the agreement. Assuring that a proper business associate agreement is executed is critical to full compliance with HIPAA.

Preemption

If a federal statute states that it preempts or overrides state laws on a particular issue, then the federal law is the law that must be followed. The HIPAA statute has a somewhat modified preemption clause. The statute provides that HIPAA overrides state laws on the protection of and access to health information, unless the state law grants the subject of the information more protection or access. So, as a general rule, HIPAA will apply. In some states there may be particular aspects of state law that give the individual more protections and/or more rights. Thus, in those states, the state law will apply to the situation. It is necessary to understand the law applicable to the situation to ensure that a privacy violation does not occur. Checking with the privacy office is a good way to learn when state law might trump HIPAA.

Penalties for Privacy Violations

- Privacy violation complaints lead to negative publicity and threaten the integrity of a covered entity.

- Unintentional violations are subject to civil penalties (up to $100 for each violation with a $25,000 annual limit).

- Intentional violations are subject to criminal penalties (up to a $50,000 fine and one year in jail; up to $250,000 and ten years in jail for selling patient information).

- Patients can file complaints directly with the Department of Health and Human Services (DHHS).

HIPAA Security Regulations

Security vs. Privacy vs. Confidentiality

The word *security* should not be confused with either *privacy* or *confidentiality*. Privacy refers to the right of an individual to control his or her personal information and to keep it from being divulged or used by others against his or her wishes. "Confidentiality" only becomes an issue once an individual's personal information has been received by another entity. Confidentiality is a means of protecting that information, usually by safeguarding it from unauthorized disclosure. Security applies to the spectrum of physical, technical and administrative safeguards put in place to protect the integrity, availability and confidentiality of information and the systems in which it is stored.

The HIPAA security regulations address the required physical, technical and administrative safeguards that must be employed by a covered entity to protect the integrity, availability, and confidentiality of electronic health information. A distinction between the security and the privacy regulations is that the security regulations only apply to PHI maintained in an electronic medium (ePHI), whereas the privacy rule applies to all PHI held by a covered entity.

Under the security regulations each safeguard is broken down into standards. The standards are in some cases further broken down into implementation specifications. The security rule either requires the standard to be implemented or defines it as addressable. If a standard is required it must be implemented as outlined in the regulation.

If an implementation specification is defined as addressable, the covered entity has several options for implementation. The covered entity can either implement the specification as defined in the regulations, implement the specification in combination with another methodology to meet the requirement, use a methodology different from that outlined in the regulation but implement the standard, or not implement the standard as specified at all. If a covered entity decides an addressable specification is not going to be implemented, the covered entity must document the rationale that led to this conclusion.

The **security rule** requires organizations to control the means by which PHI is kept confidential and to take steps to ensure that the systems that process these data are available as needed and provide reliable information. It applies to all **individually identifiable health information (IIHI)** that is stored or transmitted in electronic form.

How Do We Use Patient Information?

Caregivers need access to patient information in order to determine what services the patient needs and how to provide the best possible care. Those responsible for billing use the information to bill patients or their insurance carriers for the services they receive.

Other entities, such as quality assurance groups, need the information to make sure patients are receiving high-quality care.

What Patient Information Do You Need to Know About?

The rule requires that providers make reasonable efforts not to use or disclose more information than they need to do their jobs. So, you might ask yourself, what is the least amount of information I need to do my job?

Why Are Privacy, Confidentiality, and Security Important?

Patients have the right to control who will see their identifiable protected health information. Their expectations of privacy and confidentiality are important to providing good health care. This means that communications with and about patients involving their PHI will be limited to those who need the information for purposes related to treatment, payment, or operations.

It also means that computer systems must be managed in ways that ensure that they remain available to authorized use and that the data used to treat patients is reliable and accurate.

COMPLIANCE 101

Epilogue

EPILOGUE

As you know, better than most, compliance professionals must deal with complex and cumbersome laws and regulations on a daily basis. But health care laws and regulations are not new. Even the False Claims Act, which figures so prominently in today's discussions about Medicare compliance, dates back to the Civil War. We in health care have *always* been doing compliance. Today, more so than in the past, we are approaching compliance in a formal, systematic way. Armed with a mandate from management and guidance from the government, we are creating and implementing compliance programs—programs that embody and fulfill our organizations' commitment to compliance as part of providing the best possible heath care services.

Organizational commitment is key to an effective compliance program just as it is key to providing quality health care. Commitment not only from management but from every staff member is needed to achieve a truly effective compliance program. An environment of trust is the ultimate benefit of total organizational commitment, and that trust, in turn, is what inspires cooperation and participation from all employees. In addition, appropriate and ample educational opportunities ensure that staff have the tools to do their jobs and fulfill their responsibilities. The result is the confidence of knowing that if there are questions or if errors are discovered, employees will come forward *within* the organization.

No matter what the culture of your organization, you, as a compliance professional, whether it is compliance officer or a member of the compliance oversight committee, are charged with building or enhancing that atmosphere of trust. You must work toward that goal every day. Commitment begins with you.

Early on, we emphasized strongly that it is better to have no policy than one that is ignored. Embodied in that message is the need for constant attention. Compliance can be a demanding task master. You aren't facing it alone, however. Remember that you have, through HCCA among many other educational resources, *thousands* of colleagues with whom you can network. Use every resource available to find new ways for replenishing your own commitment and enhancing your organization's commitment.

I hope this book has provided some help and guidance for you as you launch your career in compliance. We are here to help—no matter what new challenges the future brings.

Greg Warner
Director for Compliance, Mayo Clinic

COMPLIANCE 101

Appendix

APPENDIX A ▪ Sample Letters to Vendors

Dear Vendor Colleague:

Our organization is committed to building and supporting an organization that demonstrates honesty, integrity, ethics, and best practices. In an effort to strengthen this commitment, we have established a Corporate Compliance Program and developed a Standards of Conduct. These Standards of Conduct are our attempt to offer guidance for the complex legal and business issues we face every day, and to provide the overall principles for our system. The standards outlined apply to all employees. We also expect them to apply to all our vendor, supplier, and affiliate colleagues.

Please direct your attention to the Conflicts of Interest section of the standards. You can see this standard clearly prohibits employees and their families from receiving gifts or any other consideration of value from a person or organization that does business or may want to do business with our organization or its affiliates. The only exception is a gift of nominal value extended as a business courtesy, such as sales promotion items or occasional business-related meals or entertainment of modest value. In an effort to help our employees abide by this standard, we are requesting that all vendors, suppliers and affiliates refrain from offering our employees any items other than ones of nominal value.

Thank you. If you have questions or would like to discuss the Standards for Business Conduct handbook or the Conflict of Interest standard, please do not hesitate to contact me.

Sincerely,
[Name]
Compliance Officer

Dear Vendor,

Our business partners are vital to our success, and we strive to treat each one equitably and fairly with professionalism and respect. Accordingly, our core business philosophies of quality, compliance, and ethics set forth the expectation through our "Standards of Conduct" that the hospital and its agents use prudent judgment in business transactions. This includes, but is not limited to, a policy regarding the solicitation and acceptance of gifts and entertainment which I would like to bring to your attention as outlined below. By following this policy, it allows the hospital to conduct business without the implication or perception that decisions or the resulting transactions are influenced unfairly.

- We never solicit gifts or entertainment.
- We may not accept cash or its equivalents (gift cards, gift certificates, stock, coupons, etc.).
- Any vendor or contract-sponsored travel requires prior approval of our Corporate Ethics Department.

I am asking for your assistance and cooperation in enforcing this policy. Specifically, I am requesting that food not be distributed to hospital departments or employees. If your company wishes to provide a continuing educational class for the employees, then you may provide food along with the class, but it is neither expected nor required. I would also like to ask you to limit these type of classes to once per quarter. Whenever you visit the hospital, please remember to obtain a visitors badge immediately when you arrive.

Sincerely,
[Name]
Compliance Officer

Courtesy of Cypress Fairbanks Medical Center,
Tenet Healthcare, Houston, Texas

Dear Corporate Business Partner:

As you are probably aware, the Office of the Inspector General of the United States has issued a set of corporate compliance guidelines for hospitals. Included in this plan is a requirement that all parties doing business with a given hospital must agree to abide by the hospital's code of conduct. A copy of our Code of Conduct as it relates to general business practices is enclosed for your review. Please return the enclosed statement of agreement, signed by the appropriate party, to [INSERT NAME, TITLE]. A postage paid envelope is included for your convenience.

Thank you in advance for your assistance in this matter. Feel free to contact myself or [INSERT NAME], Corporate Compliance Officer, if you need additional information.

Sincerely,
[Name]
Director, Organizational Compliance

Courtesy of Pikeville Medical Center,
Pikeville, Kentucky

APPENDIX B ▪ Sample Nonretaliation Policy

Courtesy of the University of Louisville, School of Medicine, Office of Compliance

Nonretaliation/Nonretribution Policy

Background/Purpose

- The University of Louisville School of Medicine has implemented a billing compliance program that promotes the highest standard of ethical and legal conduct. Standards of conduct and procedures for faculty members, residents, and staff are implemented to guide this effort.

- The University of Louisville School of Medicine believes that positive employee relations and morale can be achieved best and maintained in a working environment that promotes ongoing open communication between supervisors and their employees. Open and candid discussions of employee problems and concerns are encouraged.

- The University of Louisville School of Medicine believes employees should express their problems, concerns and opinions on any issue and feel that their views are important. To that end, a policy that will encourage employees to communicate problems, concerns and opinions without fear of retaliation or retribution will be implemented.

Policy

1. All employees are responsible for promptly reporting actual or potential wrongdoing, including an actual or potential violation of law, regulation, policy, or procedure.

2. The office of compliance will maintain an "open door policy" to allow individuals to report problems and concerns.

3. The office of compliance will act upon the concern promptly and in the appropriate manner.

4. The Compliance Hotline (PHONE NUMBER) is designed to permit individuals to call, anonymously or in confidence, to report problems and concerns or to seek clarification of compliance-related issues.

5. Employees who report concerns in good faith will not be subjected to retaliation, retribution, or harassment.

6. No employee is permitted to engage in retaliation, retribution or any form of harassment against another employee for reporting compliance-related concerns. Any retribution, retaliation or harassment will be met with disciplinary action.

7. Employees cannot exempt themselves from the consequences of wrongdoing by self-reporting, although self-reporting may be taken into account in determining the appropriate course of action.

Procedures

1. Knowledge of actual or potential wrongdoing, misconduct, or violations of the compliance plan must be reported immediately to management, the compliance office, or the Compliance Hotline.

2. All managers must maintain an open-door policy and take aggressive measures to assure their staff that the system truly encourages the reporting of problems and that there will be no retaliation, retribution, or harassment for doing so.

3. Departmental administrators must provide a copy of this policy to all employees.

4. A copy of the policy must be posted in every department/division.

5. If employees have concerns, they should be addressed in the following order:
   - Immediate supervisor
   - Department manager
   - Department head/director

6. If an employee feels uncomfortable with the above, the employee should report concerns directly to the Compliance Office or the Hotline.

7. All concerns will be investigated within 30 days.

8. Confidentiality regarding employee concerns and problems will be maintained at all times, insofar as legal and practical, informing only those personnel who have a need to know.

APPENDIX C ▪ Sample Policy

Courtesy of the University of Louisville School of Medicine Department of Compliance

Responding to Search Warrants

Statement

The university recognizes that the United States government has increased its scrutiny of health care providers by deliberately focusing on practices it considers fraudulent and abusive. It has a number of techniques at its disposal to use when investigating suspected fraudulent activity. Those techniques include grand jury subpoenas, civil investigative demands, civil subpoenas and search warrants. Among these techniques, the use of search warrants has grown in popularity among government investigators for a variety of reasons, thus increasing the likelihood that the university, its Office of Compliance, or other officers may be served with a search warrant. The Fourth Amendment of the U.S. Constitution guarantees people the right to be secure in their persons, papers and effects against unreasonable searches and seizures. A search may be conducted only upon a finding of probable cause. Probable cause to conduct a search is based on a review of all of the circumstances surrounding a situation and whether a reasonable person has an honest belief that the objects sought are linked to the commission of a crime, and that those objects will be found in the place to be searched and the items to be seized. The investigating officer(s) has no discretion to determine what should be seized or searched; the officer must follow the description on the face of the search warrant.

Policy

It is the policy of the university to cooperate with the government's execution of a search warrant within the bounds of the law. The university recognizes that access to an investigating officer possessing a valid search warrant cannot be refused; however, the university further recognizes that it is not legally required to relinquish all rights of ownership, or provide access to objects and areas not defined in the search warrant. The university, therefore, sets forth the following guidelines for responding to a search warrant and encourages all departmental entities to adopt this or a similar policy.

Procedure

Should the Office of Compliance or a University School of Medicine Department governed by the compliance plan receive a search warrant, the following steps shall be taken:*

1. The Director of the Office of Compliance (hereafter "Director") shall request to see the search warrant, and the affidavit of probable cause, if available. The Director shall carefully review, and copy, the search warrant and affidavit to identify the areas of the search.

2. The investigating officer(s) will be confined to the areas where the records specified in the search warrant are located. The investigating officer(s) will be given access to only those records, items and areas specified in the warrant.

3. Following the arrival of the investigating officer(s), the Director or his or her designee shall immediately notify the Dean, or his or her designee, and the university counsel.

4. The Director or his or her designee shall discharge all nonessential personnel for the day. Personnel shall be instructed that absent a subpoena directed at each individual, they are under no obligation to answer any questions asked by the investigating officer(s).

5. The Director or his or her designee shall remain with the investigating officer(s) at all times. Except to answer questions pertaining to the location of documents, or other questions wholly unrelated to the search (for example, location of copy machines, coffee machines, lavatories, etc.), the Director or designee shall not answer any questions asked by the investigating officer(s) unless counsel for the university is present.

6. Should the investigating officer(s) attempt to enter unauthorized areas or search or review documents not specified in the warrant, the Director or his or her designee shall strongly and clearly object to the investigating officer(s)' request. If the investigating officer(s) ignores the objections of the Director, the Director shall continue to object throughout the investigating officer(s)' review of the objected-to material. The compliance officer or his or her designee should carefully document the items which he or she objected to and the nature and extent of all objections.

7. The Director and/or his or her designee shall closely monitor the activity of the investigating officer(s):

    a. The investigating officer(s) should not remain alone but should be chaperoned at all times by the director or his or her designee;
    b. The investigating officer(s)' activities should be closely observed and notes made by the Director and/or his or her designee of the items and areas searched and the items seized;
    c. The Director and/or his or her designee should create a contemporaneous detailed inventory of all items or documents seized; and

d. The Director and/or his or her designee shall observe the investigating officer(s)' search only, but shall not in any way impede, assist, explain or otherwise answer questions posed by the investigating officer(s).

8. The Director and/or his or her designee shall advise the agents about what material is required in order to allow the Office of Compliance to carry out its business following the departure of the investigating officer(s). The Director and/or his or her designee shall obtain the investigating officer(s)' permission to:

a. Make copies of all documents essential to the continued conduct of business of the Office of Compliance or University School of Medicine Department prior to turning over the material to the investigating officer(s);

b. If computer files are requested as a part of the search, then copy those files prior to turning them over to the investigating officer(s); and

c. Duplicate any other material essential to the continued conduct of the business.

9. The Director and/or his or her designee shall request from the investigating officer(s) a copy of their inventory that they have created pursuant to the search and seizure. The Director and/or his or her designee shall ask that to the extent possible, if the inventory identifies the boxes and contents of boxes by numbers and documents therein, that the copy of said inventory be turned over to the Director.

10. Following the investigating officer(s)' departure from the premises, the Director and/or his or her designee shall review, with the Dean and university counsel, the inventory of items seized. University counsel, the Dean, and the Director shall formulate a plan for debriefing any employees and other university officials as soon as conveniently possible.

See Steven M. Kowal, "Execution of a Criminal Search Warrant by the FDA – Effective Preparation and Response," 52 Food Drug L.J. 117 (1997).

APPENDIX D ▪ Sample Compliance Officer Position Job Descriptions

From The Health Care Compliance Professional's Manual, *edited by R. Snell, B. Saunders. J. Murphy, E. Ryan; Aspen Health Law and Compliance Center; 1999. Aspen Publishers and HCCA. Gaithersburg, MD, and Philadelphia, PA. Reprinted with permission.*

Compliance Officer Position Job Description

The Position

The Compliance Officer provides direction and oversight of the Compliance Program. The Compliance Officer is responsible for identifying and assessing areas of compliance risk for the hospital; communicating the importance of the Compliance Program to the executive management and the Board of Directors; preparing and distributing the written Code of Conduct, setting forth the ethical principles and policies which are the basis of the Compliance Program; developing and implementing education programs addressing compliance and the Code of Conduct; implementing a retaliation-free internal reporting process, including an anonymous telephone reporting system; and collaborating with executive management to effectively incorporate the Compliance Program within system operations and programs and to carry out the responsibilities of the position.

Primary job duties and responsibilities:

- Ensuring that the Compliance Program effectively prevents and/or detects violation of law, regulations, organization policies, or the Code of Conduct.

- Regularly reviewing the Compliance Program and recommending appropriate revisions and modifications, including advising administrative leadership and the Board of Directors of potential compliance risk areas.

- Coordinating resources to ensure the ongoing effectiveness of the Compliance Program.

- Implementing and operating retaliation-free reporting channels, including an anonymous telephone reporting system available to all employees, volunteers, and affiliated providers.

- Developing educational programs for all employees, agents, affiliated providers, or others working with the hospital.

- Ensuring that the internal controls are capable of preventing and detecting significant instances or patterns of illegal, unethical, or improper conduct by employees, agents, affiliated providers, or others working with the hospital.

- Ensuring that the system has effective mechanisms to reasonably determine that persons either promoted to or hired in management and certain other sensitive and/or responsible positions (to be designated) do not have a propensity to violate federal or state laws and regulations or engage in improper or unethical conduct in their designated areas of responsibility.

- Providing input and/or direction to Human Resources policies and procedures and the performance appraisal and incentive programs to ensure that improper conduct is discouraged and that support of any conformity with the Compliance Program is part of any performance evaluation process for all employees.

- Coordinating as appropriate with outside legal counsel, conducting or authorizing and overseeing investigations of matters that merit investigation under the Compliance Program.

- Overseeing follow-up and, as applicable, resolution to investigations and other issues generated by the Compliance Program, including development of corrective action plans, as needed.

- Tracking all issues referred to the compliance office.

- Developing productive working relationships with all levels of management.

- Presenting periodic and annual reports on the Compliance Program to the Board of Directors.

- Developing and implementing, with approval of executive management and the Board, an annual review of an update to the Compliance Plan.

- Reporting on a regular basis to the Compliance Committee on matters involving the Compliance Program. Additionally, the Compliance Officer at his/her discretion is expected to regularly report issues to the CEO and Board of Directors.

- Working with administrative leadership to provide adequate information to staff to ensure that they have the requisite information and knowledge of regulatory issues and requirements to carry out their responsibilities in a lawful and ethical manner.

- Ensuring that all contracts contain language which is corporate compliant.

- Representing the Compliance Committee, including developing appropriate agendas, reports, and information as directed from by the committee.

- Performing other duties as assigned by the CEO.

Principal Duties

- Oversee, coordinate and monitor the day-to-day compliance activities of the business unit.

- In consultation with the corporate law department, establish a company compliance manual. Maintain and supplement the manual as necessary.

- Establish, supervise, and train teams of laboratory and department compliance officers responsible for identifying compliance issues at the laboratory/departmental level. Ensure appropriate communication for compliance issues between local and HQ levels.

- Develop and coordinate appropriate compliance training and education programs for all employees. Ensure and understand the company's commitment to comply with all laws, regulations, company policies, and ethical requirements applicable to the conduct of the business. Assess the need for additional training and education and develop appropriate compliance programs.

- Develop, coordinate, and/or oversee internal and external audit procedures for the purpose of monitoring and detecting any misconduct or noncompliance. If any misconduct or noncompliance is detected, recommend a solution, and follow up to ensure that the recommendations have been implemented.

- Formalize and monitor a system to enable employees to report any noncompliance without fear of retribution, ensuring that the reporting system is adequately publicized and that allegations of noncompliance are investigated and responded to promptly.

- In consultation with the Human Resources Department, help ensure that there is a mechanism in place for disciplining instances of noncompliance (including the failure to prevent, detect, or report any noncompliance), appropriate to the nature and extent of the deviation, and ensure consistency in the application of disciplinary action.

- Work with the Human Resources Department to ensure a work force with high ethical standards, including the establishment of minimum standards for conducting appropriate background and reference checks on potential employees.

- In conjunction with the Corporate Law Department, interface and, when appropriate, negotiate with external regulatory agencies.

- Report to the Compliance Committee at its regular meetings, or as otherwise necessary, on any significant compliance issues to ensure appropriate discussion of such compliance issues and to ensure that appropriate action is taken.

- Carry out all duties and responsibilities as assigned by the Compliance Committee.

Job Specifications: Education and Experience Required

Law degree preferred with experience in health care law and specific knowledge of fraud and abuse and Medicare/Medicaid issues.

- Auditing/CPA experience a plus.
- Experience in dealing with compliance issues preferred.
- Strong influencing skills and perseverance in investigating.

JOB DESCRIPTION

Vice President, Corporate Compliance

Reports to: CEO; Board of Directors
Minimum Education Level: Juris Doctor degree, Masters degree, or other post-graduate degree in a health care-related field or with appropriate experience
Performance Review: Annually

Roles and Responsibilities

The Vice President, Corporate Compliance (VPCC) will provide centralized oversight of the organization's ethics and compliance efforts generally, including the administration, investigation and enforcement of the organization's ethics and compliance plan and policies.

The VPCC will serve as a focal point for ethics and compliance program activities. Organization ethics and compliance efforts will be centralized in the office of the VPCC. The VPCC will play a crucial role in developing, implementing and maintaining an effective program. The VPCC will have direct access to all employees, including the governing board and executive management team.

The VPCC will:

- Provide leadership for the corporate ethics and compliance program (manage and oversee the organization's corporate ethics and compliance program);

- Work diligently to foster a culture and climate of sensitivity to ethical and compliant behavior within the organization;

- Identify the appropriate resources necessary to manage the ethics and compliance program and establish a budget to support such resources;

- With the ethics and compliance committee, develop and routinely review and revise, as necessary, a code of ethics and business conduct;

- Effectively communicate ethics and compliance standards to the organization's employees and contractors and vendors, as appropriate;

- Coordinate and monitor employee and board training regarding compliance with laws, regulations and corporate policies;

- Coordinate and support corporate monitoring and auditing procedures of business conduct practices (corporate staff and, as appropriate, management company personnel will be involved in this process);

- With the Senior Management, coordinate and support corporate monitoring and auditing procedures of clinical practices;

- Advise the Board of Directors, Senior Management, employees and affiliates on ethics and business conduct issues, as necessary and appropriate;

- Coordinate internal investigations of alleged violations of ethics and compliance standards;

- Review all internal compliance, audit reports and investigation reports pertaining to the organization;

- When advisable, secure opinions of outside consultants and counsel about ethics and business conduct issues with the ethics and compliance committee;

- Work with legal counsel and outside consultants, when identified, in conducting more detailed investigations, as necessary;

- Take prompt corrective actions in response to identified concerns or problems, as well as preventive actions where potentials for concern are identified;

- With the ethics and compliance committee (ECC), initiate immediate remedial actions as warranted by extreme circumstances or recommend remedial actions to the Board of Directors and Senior Management to correct unethical or non-compliant clinical or business conduct activities;

- Serve as a liaison to the organization's Board of Directors and Senior Management on ethics and compliance standards and business conduct issues; and

- Make periodic reports, as designated in the compliance policies and procedures, or as necessary, to the Board of Directors and Senior Management regarding ethics and compliance program activities.

APPENDIX E ▪ Sample Audit Review Forms

Compliance Audit Review Form

To be completed for a Compliance Program Audit, either routine or random.

Upon Completion, Please Return to: _____

Review Date: _____

Review Conducted by: _____

Process or Procedure to be Reviewed: _____

Reason: ❏ New Regulation ❏ Routine Review
       ❏ OIG Fraud Alert ❏ Random Review
       ❏ Other: _____

Site Location / Department(s): _____

Scope of Review (include sample size, with additional sheets if necessary): _____
_____
_____
_____
_____
_____

Results of Review (include any attachments): _____
_____
_____
_____
_____
_____

Specific Issues or Risks Identified: _____
_____

Has a Work Plan Been Initiated? ❏ Yes (If yes, attach copy.) ❏ No

Resolution of Issue: _____
_____
_____

Signature/Title/Date: _____

Compliance Audit Committee Standard Probe

Medical Record No.

Account No.

Date of Admission_____

Diagnostic and Procedural Coding

Were assigned diagnostic and procedural codes appropriate based on documentation in the medical record?   ❐ Yes   ❐ No   ❐ NA

If no, is a change in DRG/APC assignment indicated   ❐ Yes   ❐ No   ❐ NA

Were appropriate modifiers assigned, if indicated?   ❐ Yes   ❐ No   ❐ NA

Were appropriate condition codes assigned?   ❐ Yes   ❐ No   ❐ NA

Was a correct discharge status indicated? (IPs only)   ❐ Yes   ❐ No   ❐ NA

Comments: _____

_____

Medical Necessity

Did Outpatient diagnostics meet medical necessity?   ❐ Yes   ❐ No   ❐ NA

If not was an ABN obtained?   ❐ Yes   ❐ No   ❐ NA

Was MD queried for additional OP diagnostic info?   ❐ Yes   ❐ No   ❐ NA

Is a signed query form present in the record?   ❐ Yes   ❐ No   ❐ NA

Was the observation/inpatient stay reviewed by case management for medical necessity?   ❐ Yes   ❐ No   ❐ NA

Did the stay meet criteria?   ❐ Yes   ❐ No   ❐ NA

If indicated, was a notice of noncoverage issued?   ❐ Yes   ❐ No   ❐ NA

Did any patient type changes occur?   ❐ Yes   ❐ No   ❐ NA

If yes, were they appropriate?   ❐ Yes   ❐ No   ❐ NA

Was the MSP questionnaire completed?   ❐ Yes   ❐ No   ❐ NA

Comments: _____

_____

Documentation

Written order for all tests/procedures?   ❐ Yes   ❐ No   ❐ NA

H & P Present/Dictated within 24 hrs of Admission?   ❐ Yes   ❐ No   ❐ NA

Diagnostic test results/post procedural notes present?   ❐ Yes   ❐ No   ❐ NA

Do all documented billable procedures appear on bill? ❑ Yes ❑ No ❑ NA

Are billed items supported by documentation? ❑ Yes ❑ No ❑ NA

Preop anesthesia assessment within 48 hrs of surgery? ❑ Yes ❑ No ❑ NA

Pre final induction anesthesia assessment within 5 min. of procedure start time?
❑ Yes ❑ No ❑ NA

Post op anesthesia reassessment within 24 hrs or before OP discharge?
❑ Yes ❑ No ❑ NA

Professional fee charges supported by doc? ❑ Yes ❑ No ❑ NA

See E & M and PATH audit tools for detail.

Comments: _____

_____

Pharmacy Billing

A. Number billed RX items on detail bill _____

B. Number above items documented _____

C. Number documented RX items not billed _____

D. _____ divided by _____ = _____ % Billing Accuracy
   B + C   A + C

E. Number UB 92 HCPCS codes reviewed for correct billable unit
   conversions: _____

Comments: _____

_____

Patient Accounting

Claim Status: ❑ PreBill ❑ Postbill ❑ Paid ❑ Partial Denial ❑ Full Denial

Reason for Denial: _____

$$$ Impact of Probe Findings

Hospital Error:
PreBill Removed/Adj. charges _____ Added Charges _____

Post bill Overbilled _____ Underbilled_____

Payor Error: Overpaid _____ Underpaid _____

APPENDIX F ▪ Sample Confidentiality Statements

I understand and agree that, in connection with the performance of my duties as a member of the Compliance Oversight Committee, I will be engaged in activities of a confidential nature, including but not limited to participating in reviews and evaluations of internal examinations, evaluations and self-evaluations of the policies, practices and procedures of this organization. I further understand that, in this capacity, I will be expected to receive and/or to become privy to information of a confidential nature, including, but not limited to, medical records, documents and statistics which go to the issue of physician compliance with policies, procedures, statues and regulations, and other information of a confidential nature. I further understand that I will be called upon to evaluate such information, in part, by the application of laws, regulations and policies, as well as policies of this organization, to the information which I receive. I understand that my position as a member of this Committee is one which demands the highest trust, and that the organization's policies and procedures, as well as, in some instances, specific statues, regulations and governmental policies, protect the confidentiality of certain records and information which I will be reviewing by prohibiting their disclosure in any manner. In addition to any duty of confidentiality or non-disclosure imposed on me by specific statues, regulations and governmental policies, I agree to keep secret, and not to disclose to others nor make any personal use of whatsoever, either during my service on said Committee or at any time thereafter, of any said confidential information, and to hold any such documents and/or information, regardless of their nature, in strictest confidence. I understand that any violation of this confidentiality statement will subject me to disciplinary action, up to and including removal from this Committee and/or termination of employment. I further understand that my duty to maintain the information in confidence imposed hereunder shall survive my resignation or termination from this Committee or my termination of employment for whatever reason from this organization.

_____

Signature / Date

_____

Printed Name / Title

_____

Witness Signature / Date

Health System Confidentiality Agreement and Acknowledgement

As an employee or agent of Health System or one of its affiliated entities, I understand that I must keep confidential all information about a patient's identity, health, and/or finances [also known as protected health information (PHI)] that I may hear, see or read through my employment or agency with Health System. I agree to keep this information in confidence forever, even after I no longer work for Health System.

I understand that legal action may be taken against me if I, at any time:

■ have, use, copy or read PHI which is outside the scope of my assigned duties, or

■ give or allow access to any PHI which is not authorized or otherwise allowed by law.

I also understand that, within the scope of my assigned duties, my login ID is the equivalent of my legal signature, and I will be accountable for all representations made at log in and for all work done under my login ID. I understand that the electronic data and information stored in the computer systems are confidential patient, financial, organizational and proprietary data or information and I must treat them with the same care as data and information in the paper records.

I agree to respect and abide by all federal, state and local laws pertaining to the confidentiality of identifiable medical, personal and financial information obtained or accessed as electronic data and information. I agree to adhere to all Health System policies and procedures adopted to comply with the Health Insurance Portability and Accountability Act (HIPAA) governing the privacy, security and use of protected health information (PHI).

I will not access data for which I have no patient care, utilization review, billing or operational responsibilities for which such access is required. If I believe someone has compromised or broken the security of my login ID and password, I will immediately contact the Health System Security Officer at [PHONE NUMBER] "Help Desk" to have my password changed.

I understand that the misuse of my access to the computer systems of Health System, or of confidential information obtained, may subject me to disciplinary action up to immediate termination.

I understand that state and federal laws protect the confidentiality of this information and that I will be personally liable for any breach of these duties and may also be held criminally liable under the HIPAA privacy regulations for intentional and malicious release of identifiable health information.

__ I accept   __ I do not accept

Employee name (print) _____

Employee signature _____

Date _____

APPENDIX G ▪ Sample Compliance Line Information

Compliance Alertline Report

Date Received	Priority Level	Location	Caller ID	Issue: General Summary	Referral for Action	Action/ Follow-up Taken	Closed Date	Financial Repayment	Operating Unit	Senior Ops Manager

Sample Compliance Line Facts

Company ABC COMPLIANCE LINE FACTS

Q. *How may Company ABC employees report violations of law or Company ABC policy?*

A. All employees are required to promptly report all known or suspected violations of law or ABC policy. Employees may report violations to:

- Supervisor
- Manager
- Director
- Senior Leadership
- Director of Corporate Compliance
- Chief Compliance Officer (General Counsel)
- Company ABC Compliance Line

Management will assist you in reporting violations and facilitate getting you appropriate advice.

Q. *What is the Company ABC Compliance Line?*

A. The COMPANY ABC Compliance Line is a "hotline." It is a toll-free number (1-XXX-XXX-XXXX) at which you may report in a convenient and confidential way violations of law or COMPANY ABC policy. In order to provide excellent service, the COMPANY ABC Compliance Line is available 24 hours a day, 365 days a year.

Q. *What types of concerns should be reported to COMPANY ABC Compliance Line?*

A. Call COMPANY ABC Compliance Line to express concerns or report suspected violations related to:

- Bribes and Kickbacks
- Medicare/Medicaid Fraud and Abuse
- Conflicts of Interest
- Fraudulent Billing
- Privacy of Employee and Patient Records
- Confidentiality of COMPANY ABC Information
- Alteration or Destruction of COMPANY ABC Records or Financial Documents
- Potential Criminal Violations
- EMTALA (Emergency Medical Treatment Active Labor Act)
- Other Violations of law or COMPANY ABC Policy

Q. *What concerns should not be referred to the COMPANY ABC Compliance Line?*

A. Compliance Line is NOT to be used to report an immediate threat to person, property or environment. These conditions must immediately be reported as outlined in COMPANY ABC safety policies and procedures.

Q. *Do I have to provide my name?*

A. No. You may give your name if you desire, but it is not required. There are no recorders on the telephone lines or any devices that can identify or trace the number from which you are calling. COMPANY ABC is interested in resolving your concerns, not identifying the person reporting the issue.

Q. *How does COMPANY ABC Compliance Line work?*

A. The call will go to a contracted third party where one of its trained Communications Specialists will answer your call. The Communications Specialist will first ask how he or she can be of service. After you identify the reason for your call, detailed information will be gathered by the Communications Specialist to fully understand the purpose of your call and your concern. Reporting callers will be given a case number and an agreed upon time when the reporter may call back. A confidential and/or anonymous report will be prepared by the Communications Specialists and forwarded to the COMPANY ABC Compliance office. A staff member will initiate an appropriate review. In cases where you have chosen anonymity, the COMPANY ABC Compliance Line will be notified of the results of the review in order to respond to you by the agreed upon follow-up date.

Q. *Are callers limited in the number of times they can report?*
A. No. You may call as often as you wish to report information.

Q. *Will there be a review process after each report is made?*
A. Each report is taken seriously. Whether there is a review depends on a number of factors including the information provided, the details, documentation, if any, and COMPANY ABC policy.

Q. *What legal protection is afforded me when I call the COMPANY ABC Compliance Line?*
A. Under law and our own policy, COMPANY ABC is not allowed to make reprisals against employees who furnish good faith reports of inappropriate activities.

APPENDIX H ▪ Sample Compliance In-take Forms

Corporate Compliance Office

Compliance In-take Form
Confidential

Concern originates from:
☐ ABC Health System
☐ 123 Health System

Reporting Method used:
☐ Letter (attached)
☐ E-mail
☐ In person (drop in)
☐ Phone Call
☐ Fax

Date reported: _____ Time:_____ Received by: _____

Name of Person Reporting Concern: _____ Title:_____
    ☐ Does not wish to give name
    ☐ Requests identity to be kept in confidence

Contact Phone Number (home)_____(work)_____

Nature of Call
    ☐ Complaint
    ☐ Request for Guidance
    ☐ Informational

Site / Location of concern: _____

Relevant Information about allegation:

Was this concern reported to Compliance Office previously? (If yes, review existing file)
    Yes_____ No_____ Not Sure _____

Initial Advice or Information given to person when reporting the concern:

Does investigation need to be done by another department?
    Yes_____ No_____ (If yes, document department contact _____date routed_____

Was the concern resolved?
    Yes_____ No_____ Not Sure_____ (Concern forwarded to other department for resolution)

☐   **Concern entered into CompTrack - Paperwork filed**
☐   **Concern routed to _____ for entry in CompTrack**

Confidential   COMPANY LOGO HERE   **Attachment B: Policy # 15**

Date Reported	**Entry Form**	**Substantiated?**
	(to be stapled to the corresponding In-Take Form)	
Date Resolved		Yes or No (Circle one)

Priority (circle one): Low   Medium   High

Site (fill in the bank): _____

Circle Service/Dept below:	Description / Action:	Circle the Allegation type below:
Accounting/Controller	**Concern:**	Accounting Practices
Administration		Confidentialtiy
Behavioral Health Services		Confidentiality-Inappropriate Disclosure
Burn Center		Conflict of Interest
Business Services		Documentation,Billing,Coding
Call Center		Environmental
Cardiothoracic Services		Fraud / Theft
Chaplaincy		HR/Employee Relations
Corporate Compliance		Medical Necessity
Decision Support		Other
Diagnostic/Therapeutic		Patient Care
Education/Research	**Review:**	Patient Care - EMTALA
Education Services		Policy Violation
ER, Surgical, Trauma		Regulatory Inspection/Investigation
Facilities		Request for Guidance
Foundation/Volunteers		Safety
Geriatrics		Stark or Kickback
Health Info Services		
Health Plan		
Home Health		**Correction Action Needed?**
Human Resources		**Yes or No (Circle one)**
Information System		**(If Yes, add employee name(s)**
Internal Audit	**Response:**	**& titles below)**
Marketing/Public Rel		
Materials Mgmt		
Medical Legal		
Medical Specialties		
Medical Staff Serv		
Midwest Medical		
Neuromuscularskeletal		
Nursing Operations		
Nursing Standards		
Nutrition Services		
Other		
Pt Relations/Risk Mgmt	**Action:**	
Plant Operations		
Primary Care/Womens/Child		
Regional Community Clinics		
Reimbursement/Taxation		
Social Services		
Staffing Office		
Strategic Alignment		
System Quality		

COMPANY LOGO HERE

Concern:

Review:

Background Information:

Findings:

Miscellaneous Findings:

Conclusion:

Recommendations:

Miscellaneous Note:

Compliance Investigation Report and Case Disposition Log

Date & Method of Report: **Facility/ Location:**

Reported by: **Reported to:**

Title: **Title:**

Department: **Department:**

Alleged Violation:
☐ Fraud/Abuse   ☐ Kickback/Bribe   ☐ Stark violation   ☐ Altered Order

☐ False Documentation   ☐ Inappropriate Behavior (ethical)
☐ Billing for Non-Covered Services   ☐ Unprofessional Behavior (practice act)
☐ Billing for Services Not Provided   ☐ Other:
☐ Medicare   ☐ Medicaid
☐ Insurance/ Private Pay

Investigative Process:
☐ Clinical Record review   ☐ Staff Interview   ☐ Patient/Family Interview

☐ Personnel File Review   ☐ Review of Bill   ☐ Physician Interview

☐ Payroll Records   ☐ Other:

Documentation Reviewed:
☐ Interview Notes   ☐ Clinical Records   ☐ Physician Orders

☐ Personnel Information   ☐ Billing/Payroll   ☐ Other:_____

Witness Log: ☐ See attached log   **Documentation Attached:** ☐ See attached log   ☐ None/ In file

Detailed Incident Description (continue on separate page if necessary):

Results of Investigation:

☐ No compliance issue found   ☐ Bill adjusted: repayment $_____

☐ Employee terminated   ☐ Employee reported to Professional Board

☐ Employee written warning   ☐ Reported incident to Risk Management

☐ Employee in-service   ☐ Reported incident to Legal Services

☐ Other: _____

Incident Resolution and Follow-up:

Corrective Action

☐ Compliance Alert Issued   ☐ Compliance Training Completed on Subject

Plan Initiated:

☐ New/revised Policy   ☐ Change in Practice Initiated

Date Report Closed:

_____

By: [Name]
V.P., Corporate Compliance

_____

APPENDIX 1 ▪ Sample HIPAA-PHI Procedure

Confidentiality of Protected Health Information

Purpose

To establish a mechanism to protect the confidentiality of individually identifiable patient health and financial information from any unauthorized intentional or unintentional use or disclosure in accordance with the requirements in the HIPAA Privacy Rule (See 45 CFR 164.530).

Procedure

A. "Individually Identifiable Information"—Protected Health Information ("PHI") may not be disclosed or released without a complete and valid written authorization signed by the patient, parent, or legally authorized representative, unless 1) the use of such PHI is for purposes of treatment, payment or healthcare operations, generally, or 2) release of the PHI is specifically allowed by State or Federal law without a valid authorization.

The HIPAA Privacy Rule specifies the following 18 pieces of "Individually Identifiable Information" information that, when linked with health or medical information, constitute PHI (45 CFR 164.514):

1. Names of the individual, and relatives, employers or household members of the individual;

2. Geographic identifiers of the individual, including subdivisions smaller than a state, street addresses, city, county and precinct;

3. Zip code at any level less than the initial three digits; except if the initial 3 digits cover a geographical area of 20,000 or less people, then zip code is considered an identifier;

4. All elements of dates, except year, or dates directly related to an individual including birth date, admission date, discharge date, date of death and all ages over 89 and all elements of dates (including year) indicative of such age, except that such ages and elements may be aggregated into a single category of age 90 or older;

5. Telephone numbers;

6. Fax numbers;

7. Electronic mail addresses;

8. Social security numbers;

9. Medical record numbers;

10. Health plan beneficiary numbers;

11. Account numbers;

12. Certificate/license numbers;

13. Vehicle identifiers and serial numbers, including license plate numbers;

14. Device identifiers and serial numbers;

15. Web Universal Resource Locators (URLs);

16. Internet Protocol (IP) address numbers;

17. Biometric identifiers, including finger and voice prints;

18. Full-face photographic images and any comparable images; and

19. Any other unique identifying number, characteristic, or code;

B. "Patient"—A patient is any individual who seeks and/or receives services within the (organization name) Health System.

C. "Protected Health Information" ("PHI")-Any individually identifiable health or financial information, whether verbal, written, electronic, or otherwise recorded in any form or medium that:

1. is created or received by (organization name) or one of its affiliated entities or one of their employees, agents, or assigns, and

2. relates to the past, present, or future physical or mental health or condition of an individual; the provision of health care to an individual, or the past, present, or future payment for the provision of health care to an individual.

1. Health System, its affiliated entities, and their officers, employees, and agents are expected to treat all PHI in any form (paper, electronic, verbal, etc.) as confidential in accordance with government regulations, professional ethics, legal requirements, and accreditation standards, and they:

a. will not divulge PHI unless the patient, parent, or legally authorized representative has properly authorized the release or the release is otherwise required or permitted by law and in accordance with our policies.

b. will release only the reasonable minimum amount of information required by the requestor when a release is appropriately authorized.

c.   will take appropriate steps to prevent unauthorized re-disclosures of PHI received from sources other than records.

2. Confidentiality Statement. All employees are required to sign a confidentiality statement before they are granted access to PHI.

3. Training. All employees are required to be trained on policies and procedures regarding confidentiality and PHI to the extent necessary for each individual member to carry out their assigned functions within. This training must be documented and retained with the employee's personnel file.

    At a minimum, training will occur:

    a.   upon hire, or as quickly after hire as feasible, and

    b.   when an employee's functions or assignment of duties are changed; and/or

    c.   changes in government regulation or policies and procedures occur.

4. Sanctions. Significant unauthorized or improper release of PHI by an employee or agent may result in disciplinary action up to and including termination of employment (by organization name), civil fines and/or penalties, and/or criminal sanctions (by the government), lawsuits and judgments against the employee. Such conduct by an employee or agent may also result in civil and/or criminal fines and/or penalties against (organization name) or one of its affiliated entities (See 45 CFR 164.530 e(1) & (2)).

5. Reporting. Any employee who believes he/she has observed a violation of this policy should report it to his/her immediate supervisor, the next level of management, any other manager within (organization name) or to the HIPAA Privacy Officer at ###-###-####. An employee may also report a violation anonymously or confidentially to the Compliance AlertLine at 1-888-###-####. Calls received on this line will be referred to the Compliance Department for investigation. There will be no retaliation taken against any employee for making such a report in good faith.

APPENDIX J ▪ Code of Ethics for Health Care Compliance Professionals

Code of Ethics for Health Care Compliance Professionals
Adopted by HCCA on September 15, 1999

Preamble

Health care compliance programs are ultimately judged by how they affect, directly or indirectly, the delivery of health care to the patients, residents, and clients served by the healthcare industry and, thus, by how they contribute to the well-being of the communities we serve. Those served by the healthcare industry are particularly vulnerable, and therefore health care compliance professionals (HCCPs) understand that the services we provide require the highest standards of professionalism, integrity and competence. The following Code of Ethics expresses the profession's recognition of its responsibilities to the general public, to employers and clients, and to the legacy of the profession.

The Code of Ethics consists of two kinds of standards: Principles and Rules of Conduct. The principles are broad standards of an aspirational and inspirational nature, and as such, express ideals of exemplary professional conduct. The rules of conduct are specific standards that prescribe the minimum level of conduct expected of each HCCP. Compliance with the code is a function both of the individual professional and of the professional community. It depends primarily on the HCCP's own understanding and voluntary actions, and secondarily on reinforcement by peers and the general public.

A Commentary is provided for some rules of conduct, which is intended to clarify or elaborate the meaning and application of the rule. The following conventions are used throughout the code:

- "Employing organization" includes the employing organization and clients;

- "Law" or "laws" includes all federal, state and local laws and regulations, court orders and consent agreements, and all foreign laws and regulations that are consistent with those of the United States;

- "Misconduct" includes both illegal acts and unethical conduct; and

- "Highest governing body" of the employing organization refers to the highest policy and decision-making authority in an organization, such as the board of directors or trustees of an organization.

Principle I: Obligations to the Public

Healthcare compliance professionals should embrace the spirit and the letter of the law governing their employing organization's conduct and exemplify the highest ethical standards in their conduct in order to contribute to the public good.

R1.1   HCCPs shall not aid, abet or participate in misconduct.

R1.2   HCCPs shall take such steps as are necessary to prevent misconduct by their employing organizations.

R1.3   HCCPs shall exercise sound judgement in cooperating with all official and legitimate government investigations of, or inquiries concerning, their employing organization.

> *Commentary: While the role of the HCCP in a government investigation may vary, the HCCP shall never obstruct or lie in an investigation*

R1.4   If, in the course of their work, HCCPs become aware of any decision by their employing organization which, if implemented, would constitute misconduct, adversely affect the health of patients, residents or clients, or defraud the system, the professional shall: (a) refuse to consent to the decision; (b) escalate to the highest governing authority, as appropriate; (c) if serious issues remain unresolved after exercising "a" and "b", consider resignation; and (d) report the decision to public officials when required by law.

> *Commentary: The duty of a compliance professional goes beyond other professionals in an organizational context, inasmuch as his/her duty to the public includes prevention of organizational misconduct. The compliance professional should exhaust all internal means available to deter his/her employing organization, its employees, and its agents from engaging in misconduct. HCCPs should consider resignation only as a last resort, since compliance professionals may be the only remaining barrier to misconduct. In the event that resignation becomes necessary, however, the duty to the public takes priority over any duty of confidentiality to the employing organization. A letter of resignation should set forth to senior management and the highest governing body of the employing organization the precise conditions that necessitate his/her action. In complex organizations, the highest governing body may be the highest governing body of a parent corporation.*
>
> *The steps of resignation and government notification are typically only appropriate if: (1) the compliance officer has detected a course of action that*

is a certain, serious, and material violation of the law: (2) the health care compliance professional has made the most energetic of efforts internally to surface and resolve the matter: and (3) the management of the organization, including at the highest levels, declines to take any remedial action and does so in apparent recognition that the course of action which the compliance officer seeks to correct is in violation of the law.

Principle II: Obligations to the Employing Organization

Health care compliance professionals should serve their employing organizations with the highest sense of integrity, exercise unprejudiced and unbiased judgment on their behalf, and promote effective compliance programs.

R2.1 HCCPs shall serve their employing organizations in a timely, competent and professional manner.

> ***Commentary:*** *HCCPs are not expected to be experts in every field of knowledge that may contribute to an effective compliance practice in the healthcare industry. HCCPs venturing into areas that require additional expertise shall obtain that expertise by additional education, training, or through the retention of others with such expertise. HCCPs shall also have current and general knowledge of all relevant fields of knowledge that reasonably might be expected of a health care compliance professional, and shall take steps to ensure that they remain current by pursuing opportunities for continuing education and professional development.*

R2.2 HCCPs shall ensure to the best of their abilities that employing organizations comply with all relevant laws.

> ***Commentary:*** *While HCCPs should exercise a leadership role in compliance assurance, all employees have the responsibility to ensure compliance.*

R2.3 HCCPs shall investigate with appropriate due diligence all issues, information, reports and/or conduct that relate to actual or suspected misconduct, whether past, current or prospective.

R2.4 HCCPs shall keep senior management and the highest governing body informed of the status of the compliance program, both as to the implementation of the program, and about areas of compliance risk.

> ***Commentary:*** *The HCCP's ethical duty under this rule complements the duty of senior management and the highest governing body to assure themselves "that information and reporting systems exist in the organization that are reasonably designed to provide to senior management and to the board itself, timely, accurate information sufficient to allow management and the*

board, each within its scope, to reach informed judgments concerning both the corporation's compliance with law and its business performance." In re Caremark International Inc., Derivative Litigation,1996 WL 549894, at 8 (Del. Ch. Sept. 25, 1996).

R2.5 HCCPs shall not aid or abet retaliation against any employee who reports actual, potential or suspected misconduct, and they shall strive to implement procedures that ensure the protection from retaliation against any employee who reports actual, potential or suspected misconduct.

Commentary: HCCPs should preserve, to the best of their ability, consistent with other duties imposed on them by this Code of Ethics, the anonymity of reporting employees, if such employees request anonymity. Further, they shall conduct the investigation of any actual, potential or suspected misconduct with utmost discretion, being careful to protect the reputations and identities of those being investigated.

R2.6 HCCPs shall not reveal confidential information obtained in the course of their professional activities, recognizing that under certain circumstances confidentiality must yield to other values or concerns, e.g., to stop an act which creates appreciable risk to health and safety, or to reveal a confidence when necessary to comply with a subpoena or other legal process.

Commentary: It is not necessary to reveal confidential information to comply with a subpoena or legal process if the communications are protected by a legally recognized privilege (e.g., attorney-client privilege).

R2.7 HCCPs shall take care to avoid any actual, potential, or perceived conflict of interest; to disclose them when they cannot be avoided; and to remove them where possible. Conflicts of interest can also create divided loyalties. HCCPs shall not permit loyalty to individuals in the employing organization with whom they have developed a professional or a personal relationship to interfere with or supersede the duty of loyalty to the employing organization and/or the superior responsibility of upholding the law, ethical business conduct, and this Code of Ethics.

Commentary: If HCCPs have any business association, direct or indirect financial interest, or other interest which could be substantial enough to influence their judgment in connection with their performance as a professional, the HCCPs shall fully disclose to their employing organizations the nature of the business association, financial interest, or other interest. If a report, investigation, or inquiry into misconduct relates directly or indirectly to activity in which the HCCP was involved in any manner, the HCCP must disclose in writing the precise nature of that involvement to the senior management of the employing organization before responding to a report or beginning an investigation or inquiry into such matter. Despite this requirement, such involvement in a matter subject to a report, investigation or inquiry will not necessarily prejudice the HCCP's ability to fulfill his/her responsibilities in that regard.

R2.8 HCCPs shall not mislead employing organizations about the results that can be achieved through the use of their services.

Principle III: Obligations to the Profession

Compliance professionals should strive, through their actions, to uphold the integrity and dignity of the profession, to advance the effectiveness of compliance programs and to promote professionalism in health care compliance.

R3.1 HCCPs shall pursue their professional activities, including investigations of misconduct, with honesty, fairness, and diligence.

> ***Commentary:*** *HCCPs shall not agree to unreasonable limits that would interfere with their professional, ethical, and legal responsibilities. Reasonable limits include those that are imposed by the employing organization's resources. If management of the employing organization requests an investigation but limits access to relevant information, HCCPs shall decline the assignment and provide an explanation to the highest governing authority of the employing organization. The compliance professional should, with diligence, strive to promote the most effective means to achieve compliance.*

R3.2 Consistent with paragraph R2.6, HCCPs shall not disclose without consent confidential information about the business affairs or technical processes of any present or former employing organization that would erode trust in the profession or impair the ability of compliance professionals to obtain such information from others in the future.

> ***Commentary:*** *Compliance professionals need free access to information to function effectively, as well as the ability to communicate openly with any employee or agent of an employing organization. Open communication depends upon trust. Misuse and abuse of the work product of compliance professionals poses the greatest threat to compliance programs. When adversaries in litigation use an organization's own self-policing work against it, this can undermine the credibility of compliance professionals. HCCPs are encouraged to work with legal counsel to protect confidentiality and to minimize litigation risks.*

R3.3 HCCPs shall not make misleading, deceptive, or false statements or claims about their professional qualifications, experience, or performance.

R3.4 HCCPs shall not attempt to damage, maliciously or falsely, directly or indirectly, the professional reputation, prospects, practice or employment opportunities of other compliance professionals.

R3.5 HCCPs shall maintain their competence with respect to developments within the profession, including knowledge of and familiarity with current theories, industry practices, and laws.

Commentary: *HCCPs shall pursue a reasonable and appropriate course of continuing education, including, but not limited to, review of relevant professional and healthcare industry journals and publications, communication with professional colleagues, and participation in open professional dialogues and exchanges through attendance at conferences and membership in professional associations.*

COMPLIANCE 101

Glossary

GLOSSARY OF COMPLIANCE TERMS

ANTI-KICKBACK LAW: Prohibits the solicitation, receiving, offering, or paying of any remuneration, directly or indirectly, in cash or in kind, in exchange for a Medicare or Medicaid referral.

ATTESTATION: The affirmation by signature, usually on a printed form, that the action outlined has been accomplished by the individual signing; e.g., the individual has read the Code of Conduct and agreed to adhere to its principles.

ATTORNEY-CLIENT PRIVILEGE: A legally accepted policy that communication between a client and attorney is confidential in the course of the professional relationship and that such communication cannot be disclosed without the consent of the client. Its purpose is to encourage full and frank communication between attorneys and their clients.

AUDIT, BASELINE: A systematic inspection of records, policies, and procedures with the goal of establishing a set of benchmarks for comparison for future inspections.

AUDIT, CONCURRENT: An ongoing inspection of records, policies, and procedures at a given point in time in which identified potential problems are investigated as they arise (e.g., pre-billed records).

AUDIT, RETROSPECTIVE: A comprehensive inspection of records, policies, and procedures done usually in anticipation of launching a compliance program. All potential problems are identified and then investigated (e.g., post-billed, historical audit).

BALANCED BUDGET ACT OF 1997: Legislation containing major reform of the Medicare and Medicaid programs especially in the areas of home health and patient transfers. It also mandated permanent exclusion from participation in federally funded health care programs of those convicted of three health care-related crimes (3 strikes and you're out).

BENCHMARKING: The measurement of performance against "best practice" standards.

BEST PRACTICES: Generally recognized superior performance by organizations in operational and/or clinical process.

BUSINESS ASSOCIATE: is a person or organization that performs or assists in the performance of a function or activity involving the use or disclosure of individually identifiable health information on behalf of a covered entity or provides services such as legal, actuarial, accounting, consulting, data aggregation, management administration, accreditation or financial services to or for a covered entity.

CAREMARK INTERNATIONAL DERIVATIVE LITIGATION: The 1996 civil settlement of Caremark International, Inc. in which the OIG-imposed corporate integrity agreement precluded Caremark from providing health care in certain forms for a period of five years. Also suggests that the failure of a corporate Director to attempt in good faith to institute a compliance program in certain situations may be a breach of a Director's fiduciary obligation.

CENTERS FOR MEDICARE & MEDICAID SERVICES (CMS): A component of the U.S. Department of Health and Human Services that administers the Medicare, Medicaid and State Children's Health Insurance programs.

CERTIFIED PROFESSIONAL CODER (CPC): A coder who has satisfied certification requirements as established by the American Academy of Professional Coders.

CHAIN OF COMMAND: The hierarchy of reporting structure within an organization, which assumes all issues will be presented first to one's immediate supervisor.

CIVIL MONETARY PENALTIES LAW (CMPL): Regulations which apply to any claim for an item or service that was not provided as claimed or that was knowingly submitted as false, and which provides guidelines for the levying of fines for such offences.

COMPLIANCE: Adherence to the requirements of the Medicare and Medicaid laws and regulations and as stated in the Social Security Act and the regulations administered by the Centers for Medicare & Medicaid Services (CMS) and other federal and state agencies. Also: Corporate Compliance

CORPORATE INTEGRITY AGREEMENT (CIA): A negotiated settlement between a health care provider and the government in which the provider accepts no liability but must agree to implement a strict plan of government-supervised corrective action. Also: Consent Decrees

COVERED ENTITIES: (1) Health plan; (2) Health care clearinghouse; or (3) Health care provider who transmits any health information in electronic form in connection with a transaction covered by this subchapter.

Culpability Score: Part of the U.S. Sentencing Commission guidelines for the Sentencing of Organizations, a system that adds points for aggravating factors and subtracts points for mitigating factors in the determination of fines imposed for fraud or abuse.

Cumulative Sanction Report: An Internet-based, OIG-produced report listing health care providers who have been excluded from participation in the Medicare and Medicaid programs.

Current Procedural Terminology 2000 (CPT 2000): A publication of the American Medical Association which lists and assigns codes to procedures and services performed by physicians.

Designated Record Set:

1. A group of records maintained by or for a covered entity, that is:

   i. The medical records and billing records about individuals maintained by or for the covered health care provider

   ii. The enrollment, payment, claims adjudication and case or medical management records systems maintained by or for a health plan

   iii. Used, in whole or in part, by or for the covered entity to make decisions about individuals

2. For purposes of this paragraph, the term record means any item, collection, or grouping of information that includes protected health information and is maintained, collected, used or disseminated by or for a covered entity.

Diagnosis-Related Groups (DRGs): Classifications of diagnoses determined by the average cost of treating a particular condition, regardless of the number of services rendered or the length of patient stay; Medicare reimbursement is assigned by DRG.

DRG Creep: Illegal practice of intentionally billing using a DRG which provides a higher payment rate than the DRG that accurately reflects the diagnosis and treatment actually provided.

Disclosure: The release, transfer, provision of, access to, or divulging in any other manner of information outside the entity holding the information.

Employee Retirement Income Security Act (ERISA): A 1974 federal act that exempts self-insured health plans from state laws governing health insurance and requires health plans to provide certain information to enrollees.

EQUAL EMPLOYMENT OPPORTUNITY COMMISSION (EEOC): U.S. agency created in 1964 to end discrimination based on race, religion, sex or national origin in employment. The commission reviews and investigates charges of discrimination and, if found to be true, attempts remedy through conciliation or legal means.

FALSE CLAIMS ACT (FCA): Originally adopted in 1863 during the Civil War to discourage suppliers from overcharging the federal government, legislation that prohibits anyone from knowingly submitting or causing to be submitted a false or fraudulent claim.

FEDERAL SENTENCING GUIDELINES: Guidelines developed by the U.S. Sentencing Commission, an independent agency in the judicial branch of government established by the 1984 Sentencing Reform Act, to govern the sentencing of individual defendants (1987) and organizations (1991).

FISCAL INTERMEDIARY, OR FIDUCIARY INTERMEDIARY: A person or organization that, under agreement with HHS under part A of Medicare, processes claims, provides services, and issues payments on behalf of private, federal, and state health benefit programs or other insurance organizations.

GENERAL SERVICES ADMINISTRATION (GSA): The federal agency that manages the federal government's property and records, including the construction and operation of buildings and procurement and distribution of supplies, among other functions.

HEALTH AND HUMAN SERVICES (HHS); DEPARTMENT OF HEALTH AND HUMAN SERVICES: The department of the executive branch of the U.S. government with health care accountabilities, including responsibility for the Public Health Service, the Centers for Medicare & Medicaid Services (CMS) and the Social Security Administration.

HEALTH CARE: Care, services or supplies related to the health of an individual, including but not limited to: (1) Preventative, diagnostic, rehabilitative, maintenance, or palliative care, counseling, service, assessment or procedure with respect to a physical or mental condition, or functional status of an individual or affecting the structure or function of the body; and (2) Sale or dispensing of a drug, device, equipment, or other item pursuant to a prescription.

HEALTH CARE CLEARINGHOUSE: A public or private entity, including a billing service, repricing company, community health management information system or community health information system, and "value-added" networks and switches, that does either of the following functions: (1) Processes or facilitates the processing of health information received from another entity in a nonstandard format or containing nonstandard data content into standard data elements or a standard transaction; (2) Receives a standard transaction from another entity and processes or facilitates the processing of health information into nonstandard format or nonstandard data content for the receiving entity.

HEALTH CARE COMPLIANCE ASSOCIATION (HCCA): The professional association dedicated to helping health care compliance professionals, through education, networking opportunities and other resources, create an ethical environment within their organizations and meet all legal and regulatory requirements related to Medicare reimbursement.

HEALTH CARE OPERATIONS: Any of the following activities of the covered entity to the extent that the activities relate to covered functions:

1. Conducting quality assessment and improvement activities, including outcomes evaluation and development of clinical guidelines, provided that the obtaining of generalizable knowledge is not the primary purpose of any studies resulting from such activities; population-based activities relating to improving health or reducing health care costs, protocol development, case management and care coordination, contacting of health care providers and patients with information about treatment alternatives; and related functions that do not include treatment;

2. Reviewing the competence or qualifications of health care professionals, evaluating practitioner and provider performance, health plan performance, conducting training programs in which students, trainees, or practitioners in areas of health care learn under supervision to practice or improve their skills as health care providers, training of non-health care professionals, accreditation, certification, licensing, or credentialing activities;

3. Underwriting, premium rating, and other activities relating to the creation, renewal or replacement of a contract of health insurance or health benefits, and ceding, securing, or placing a contract for reinsurance of risk relating to claims for health care (including stop-loss insurance and excess of loss insurance), provided that the requirements of 164.514(g) are met, if applicable;

4. Conducting or arranging for medical review, legal services, and auditing functions, including fraud and abuse detection and compliance programs;

5. Business planning and development, such as conducting cost-management and planning-related analyses related to managing and operating the entity, including formulary development and administration, development or improvement of methods of payment or coverage policies; and

6. Business management and general administrative activities of the entity, including, but not limited to:

   a. Management activities relating to implementation of and compliance with the requirements of this subchapter;

   b. Customer service, including the provision of data analyses for policy holders, plan sponsors, or other customers, provided that protected health information is not disclosed to such policy holder, plan sponsor, or customer.

   c. Resolution of internal grievances;

   d. The sale, transfer, merger, or consolidation of all or part of the covered entity with another covered entity, or an entity that, following such activity, will become a covered entity, and due diligence related to such activity; and

   e. Consistent with the applicable requirements of 164.514, creating de-identified health information or a limited data set, and fundraising

HEALTH CARE PROVIDER: A provider of services (as defined in section 1861(u) of the Act, 42 U.S.C. 1395x(u)), a provider of medical or health services (as defined in section 1861(s) of the Act, 42 U.S.C. 1395x(s)), and any other person or organization who furnishes, bills, or is paid for, health care services or supplies in the normal course of business.

HEALTH INFORMATION: Any information, oral or recorded, in any form or medium, that:

1. is created or received by a health care provider, health plan, public health authority, employer, life insurer, school or university, or health care clearinghouse; and

2. related to the past, present, or future physical or mental health or condition of an individual; the provision of health care to an individual; or the past, present, or future payment for the provision of health care to an individual.

HEALTH INSURANCE PORTABILITY AND ACCOUNTABILITY ACT OF 1996 (HIPAA): Comprehensive legislation that ensures access to health coverage for those who change jobs or are temporarily out of work. It also provides the mechanism for funding the Department of Justice and the FBI for Medicare fraud investigations.

HEALTH PLAN: An individual or group plan that provides, or pays the cost of, medical care (as defined in section 2791(a)(2) of the PHS Act, 42 U.S.C. 300gg-91(a)(2)) of the Act.

1. A health plan includes the following singly or in combination:

    i. A group health plan, as defined in this section.

    ii. A health insurance issuer, as defined in this section.

    ii. An HMO, as defined in this section.

    iv. Part A and B of the Medicare program under title XVIII of the Act.

    v. The Medicaid program under title XIX of the Act.

    vi. An issuer of a Medicare supplemental policy.

    vii. An issuer of a long-term care policy, excluding a nursing home fixed-indemnity policy.

    viii. An employee welfare benefit plan or any other arrangement that is established or maintained for the purpose of offering or providing health benefits to the employees of two or more employers.

    ix. The health care program for active military personnel under title 10 of the United States Code.

    x. The veterans' health care program under 38 U.S.C. chapter 17. (xi) CHAMPUS.

    xii. The Indian Health Services program.

    xiii. The Federal Employees Health Benefits Program.

    xiv. An approved child State health plan under title XXI of the Act.

    xv. The Medicare + Choice program.

    xvi. A high risk pool established under State law to provide health insurance coverage or comparable coverage to eligible individuals.

xvii. Any other individual or group plan, or combination of individual or group plans, that provides or pays for the costs of medical care.

2. A Health plan excludes:

i. Any policy, plan or program to the extent that it provides, or pays for the cost of excepted benefits that are listed in section 2791(c)(1) of the PHS Act, 42 U.S.C. 300gg-91(c)(1); and

ii. A government funded program (other than one listed in paragraph (1)(i)-(xvi) of this definition);

a. Whose principal purpose is other than providing, or paying the cost of, health care; or

b. Whose principal activity is:

1. The direct provision of health care to persons; or

2. The making of grants to fund the direct provision of health care to persons.

HOTLINE; HELPLINE: A common reporting system, administered in-house or by outside consultants, giving anonymous telephone access to employees seeking to report possible instances of wrongdoing.

ICD-9-CM; INTERNATIONAL CLASSIFICATION OF DISEASES, 9TH EDITION, CLINICAL MODIFICATION: A two-part classification system in current use for coding patient medical information and for classifying patients into diagnosis-related groups (DRGs) for Medicare and other third-party payers. The first part provides a comprehensive list of diseases with corresponding codes compatible with the World Health Organization's list of diseases codes. The second part contains procedure codes independent of the disease codes. Published by the Commission on Professional and Hospital Activities (CPHA) and by the federal government.

INDIVIDUALLY IDENTIFIABLE HEALTH INFORMATION (IIHI): Information that is a subset of health information, including demographic information collected from an individual, and:

1. is created or received by a health care provider, health plan, employer, health care clearinghouse; and

2. related to the past, present or future physical or mental health or condition of an individual; the provision of health care to an individual; or the past, present or future payment for the provision of health care to an individual; and

i. That identifies the individual; or

ii. With respect to which there is a reasonable basis to believe that the information can be used to identify the individual.

INSPECTOR GENERAL (IG): An officer of a federal agency whose primary function is to conduct and supervise audits and investigations relating to operations and procedures over which the agency has jurisdiction.

JOINT COMMISSION ON ACCREDITATION OF HEALTHCARE ORGANIZATIONS (JCAHO): A not-for-profit organization that develops standards and performance measures, conducts regular on-site surveys based on those standards and measures, and awards accreditation decisions for hospitals and other health care facilities.

OCCUPATIONAL SAFETY AND HEALTH ADMINISTRATION (OSHA): A component of the Department of Labor that develops and administers standards relating to the well-being of workers at the job site, develops and issues regulations in this area, conducts investigations and inspections to determine status of compliance with safety and health standards and regulations, and issues citations and proposes penalties for noncompliance.

OIG: Office of the Inspector General

OIG COMPLIANCE PROGRAM GUIDANCES: Guidelines issued by the Office of the Inspector General for the suggested development of compliance programs. To date, seven compliance program guidances have been issued for hospitals, home health agencies, clinical laboratories, third-party billers, the durable medical equipment, prosthetics, orthotics and supply industry; hospice providers, physician practices and Medicare+Choice organizations. Individual and Small Group Physician Practices has been published for public comment. The next guidance to be issued will address compliance measures in the nursing home industry.

PAYMENT:

1. Activities undertaken by:

   i. A health plan to obtain premiums or to determine or fulfill its responsibility for coverage and provisions of benefits under the health plan; or

   ii. A health care provider or health plan to obtain or provide reimbursement for the provision of health care; and

2. The activities in paragraph (1) of this definition relate to the individual to whom health care is provided and include, but are not limited to:

i. Determinations of eligibility or coverage (including coordination of benefits or the determination of cost sharing amounts), and adjudication or subrogation of health benefit claims;

ii. Risk adjusting amounts due based on enrollee health status and demographic characteristics;

iii. Billing, claims management, collection activities, obtaining payment under a contract for reinsurance (including stop-loss insurance and excess of loss insurance), and related health care data processing;

iv. Review of health care services with respect to medical necessity, coverage under a health plan, appropriateness of care, or justification of charges

v. Utilization review activities, including precertification and preauthorization of services, concurrent or retrospective review of services; and

vi. Disclosure to consumer reporting agencies of any of the following protected health information relating to collection of premiums or reimbursement;

    a. Name and address;

    b. Date of birth;

    c. Social Security Number;

    d. Payment history;

    e. Account number; and

    f. Name and address of the health care provider and/or health plan.

PHYSICIANS AT TEACHING HOSPITALS (PATH): An HHS/OIG nationwide review of compliance with rules governing physicians at teaching hospitals. Records were reviewed to determine adequate physician involvement in patient care according to IL373, the Medicare rule that dictates that an attending physician must be present when supervising an intern or resident in order to bill for the care provided by the intern or the resident.

PROSPECTIVE PAYMENT SYSTEM (PPS): The system for paying for services for Medicare patients (see DRGs) whereby patients are classified into categories for which prices are negotiated or determined in advance.

PROTECTED HEALTH INFORMATION (PHI): Individually identifiable health information:

1. Except as provided in paragraph (2) of this definition, that is:

    i. Transmitted by electronic media;

    ii. Maintained in any medium described in the definition of electronic media at 162.103 of this subchapter; or

    iii. Transmitted or maintained in any other form or media.

2. PHI excludes IIHI in:

    i. Education records covered by FERPA;

    ii. Records described at 20 U.S.C. 1232g(a)(4)(B)(iv); and

    iii. Employment records held by a covered entity in this role as an employer.

3. That is or has been electronically maintained or electronically transmitted by a covered entity, or transmitted or maintained in any other form or media.

QUI TAM: Authorized by the False Claims Act, qui tam is an abbreviated term for "qui tam pro domino rege quam pro se ipso in hac parte sequitur," or "he who brings the action for the king as well as for himself." A qui tam suit is one filed by an employee of an organization, a whistleblower, with the federal government accusing an organization of fraud and abuse.

SAFE HARBORS: Explicit regulatory exceptions to otherwise legally prohibited conduct. Federal safe harbor regulations specify certain joint ventures and other arrangements concerning hospitals and/or physicians which do not violate Medicare fraud and abuse laws.

SELF-REFERRAL STATUTE; STARK LAW: The Omnibus Budget Reconciliation Act of 1989 (OBRA) bans physicians from referring lab specimens to any entity with which the physician has a financial relationship. Amended by OBRA90 to exclude financial relationships between hospitals and physicians unrelated to clinical laboratory services. OBRA93 (Stark II) expanded to include 10 other designated health care services.

SELF-REPORTING: Having identified actual wrongdoing, the organization informs the OIG. Although not protected from civil or criminal action under the False Claims Act, providers disclosing fraud are advised in the OIG Self-Disclosure Protocol that timely self-reporting of wrongdoing may offer mitigating factors in potential penalties and/or fines.

SEVEN ELEMENTS: Based on the seven steps of the Federal Sentencing Guidelines, each OIG corporate compliance guidance urges a formal commitment by the hospital's governing body to include all of applicable elements. They are:

1. The organization must have established compliance standards and procedures to be followed by its employees and other agents that are reasonably capable of reducing the prospect of criminal conduct.

2. Specific individual(s) within high-level personnel of the organization must have been assigned overall responsibility to oversee compliance with such standards and procedures.

3. The organization must have used due care not to delegate substantial discretionary authority to individuals whom the organization knew, or should have known through the exercise of due diligence, had a propensity to engage in illegal activities.

4. The organization must have taken steps to communicate effectively its standards and procedures to all employees and other agents, e.g., by requiring participation in training programs or by disseminating publications that explain in a practical manner what is required.

5. The organization must have taken reasonable steps to achieve compliance with its standards, e.g., by utilizing monitoring and auditing systems reasonably designed to detect criminal conduct by its employees and other agents and by having in place and publicizing a reporting system whereby employees and other agents could report criminal conduct by others within the organization without fear of retribution.

6. The standards must have been consistently enforced through appropriate disciplinary mechanisms, including, as appropriate, discipline of individuals responsible for the failure to detect an offense. Adequate discipline of individuals responsible for an offense is a necessary component of enforcement; however, the form of discipline that will be appropriate will be case specific.

7. After an offense has been detected, the organization must have taken all reasonable steps to respond appropriately to the offense and to prevent further similar offenses, including any necessary modifications to its program to prevent and detect violations of law.

SNAPSHOT: The OIG guidances suggest that at inception of a compliance program, a review of operations from a compliance perspective be done in order to judge progress in reducing or eliminating potential areas of vulnerability.

STARK LAW: See *Self-referral Statutes*.

TREATMENT: The provision, coordination, or management of health care and related services by one or more health care providers, including the coordination or management of health care by a health care provider with a third party; consultations between health care providers relating to a patient; or the referral of a patient for health care from one health care provider to another.

UNBUNDLING: The illegal practice of submitting claims individually in order to maximize reimbursement for various tests or procedures which are required to be billed together. The government initiative investigating this issue is Project Bad Bundle.

UPCODING: Coding for a higher level than the documentation warrants.

USE: With respect to individually identifiable health information, the sharing, employment, application, utilization, examination, or analysis of such information within an entity that maintains such information.

VOLUNTARY DISCLOSURE: See *Self-Reporting*.

WORKFORCE: Employees, volunteers, trainees, and other persons whose conduct, in the performance of work for the covered entity, is under the direct control of such entity, whether or not they are paid by the covered entity.

COMPLIANCE 101

Endnotes

Endnotes

1. OIG DHHS, *Compliance Program Guidance for Hospitals*, U.S. Department of Health and Human Services, 1998, p. 7.

2. Ibid, p. 2.

3. OIG DHHS, *Compliance Program Guidance for Third Party Medical Billing Companies*, U.S. Department of Health and Human Services, 1999, p. 6.

4. Ibid, p. 9.

5. Heath Care Compliance Association, *Survey of Compliance Officers*, HCCA, 2000, pp 5-10.

6. OIG DHHS, *Compliance Program Guidance for Hospitals*, U.S. Department of Health and Human Services, 1998, p. 34.

7. Ibid., p. 34.

8. OIG DHHS, *Compliance Program Guidance for Third Party Medical Billing Companies*, U.S. Department of Health and Human Services, 1999, p. 10.

9. R. Russo, *The Journal of Health Care Compliance*, 1:2. (Reprinted with permission.)

10. OIG DHHHS, *Compliance Program Guidance for Clinical Laboratories*, U.S. Department of Health and Human Services, 1998, p. 22.

11. Angela Brown, 1999 HCCA Compliance Institute, Chicago, IL (with permission).

12. OIG DHHS, *Compliance Program Guidance for Third Party Medical Billing Companies*, U.S. Department of Health and Human Services, 1999, p. 13.

13. Ibid., p. 22.

14. OIG DHHS, *Compliance Program Guidance for Home Health Agencies*, U.S. Department of Health and Human Services, 1999, p. 46.

15. OIG DHHS, *Compliance Program Guidance for Hospitals*, U.S. Department of Health and Human Services, 1998, p. 40.

16. Ibid, p. 41.

17. Ibid., p. 47.

18. OIG DHHS, *Compliance Program Guidance for Third Party Medical Billing Companies*, U.S. Department of Health and Human Services, 1999, p. 14

19. M. Meyers, "Getting Physicians on Board with your Compliance Program." *Today's Corporate Compliance*, 1:6 pp. 6-7.

20. C. Ideker, "How much should you spend on Compliance Programs," *Today's Corporate Compliance*, 1:3 pp. 6-7.

21. Ibid.

22. OIG DHHS, *Compliance Program Guidance for Hospitals*, U.S. Department of Health and Human Services, 1998, p. 43.

23. OIG DHHS, *Compliance Program Guidance for Third Party Medical Billing Companies*, U.S. Department of Health and Human Services, 1999, p. 22.

24. Ibid.

25. W. Altmann, "Six Steps to Building a Framework for Effectiveness," *Journal of Health Care Compliance*, 2:3 (reprinted with permission).